Introduction To Teaching

T. M. Stinnett
William H. Drummond
Alice W. Garry

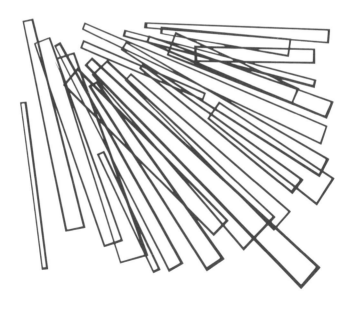

Charles A. Jones Publishing Company
Worthington, Ohio

1 2 3 4 5 6 7 8 9 10 / 79 78 77 76

Library of Congress Catalog Card Number: 74-79556
International Standard Book Number: 0-8396-0047-X

Printed in the United States of America

To me, a teacher is a person with a touch of
immortality . . . . The desire to teach is a
deep-seated one and permeates the hearts and
souls of thousands upon thousands who have
never given conscious thought to entering the
profession. We all teach in one way or another,
and in such activities we find universal and
mysterious satisfaction . . . . Why does this
happen? Because we all sense, directly or
indirectly, consciously or unconsciously, that to
leave a vestige of oneself in the development
of another is a touch of immortality.

Samuel B. Gould

Preface

Today, there is a surplus of classroom teachers in many subject fields and in most sections of the country. For the foreseeable future, the education college graduate will enter a competitive job market.

What does this mean to you if you are considering a major in education? First, you must begin your preparation early in your college years. Second, you must recognize that choosing a career in education demands as realistic an appraisal of strengths and weaknesses as choosing a career in other professions, perhaps an even more realistic one. But, you should also be aware that positions are available for the competent and well-prepared. You have a better chance than your predecessors had to match your special interests and abilities to a career in education, either as a classroom teacher or in new supportive roles.

In spite of the fact that the number of openings in elementary and secondary schools has levelled off with the national decline in birth rates and consequent decrease in enrollments, new types of school employment have developed. A greater variety of programs and services are being offered because more children with more diversified needs are staying in school until they graduate. As the average educational level of the people increases, the demand for more specialized schooling will also increase.

This book was written to give you an opportunity to examine the work of the classroom teacher so you may decide early in your college years if this is the field for you. The book suggests ways that you can begin now to explore the life of a teacher and gather firsthand observations of public and private school employment. It examines the job possibilities available in the light of the dwindling demand. But, most importantly it explores the characteristics and qualities that are found in successful classroom teachers.

This book gives you the facts about teaching, both the advantages and the disadvantages, as fairly as we can. We, of course, are optimistic about the future in education and we believe that teaching offers magnificent personal rewards. You, of course, will have to decide for yourself. That is what this book is about: to help you in answering your questions about your future in the field of education.

T. M. Stinnett
William H. Drummond
Alice W. Garry

Contents

Introduction To Teaching

Teaching as a Career

The choice of a career is a tough decision to make, especially so if you see such a decision as lifelong and irreversible. Our folklore and cultural traditions could lead you to believe that, at one point in your life, you must make up your mind about what you want to be and pursue that career interest without question or hesitancy from that point forward. But two observations militate against such a simplistic view of career choice: (1) the growth of technology and specialization and (2) the way a person's choices and experiences influence later choices and experiences.

In our highly technological society, there are thousands of occupations to choose from, and the number and kind change from year to year. Just in the field of education, for example, ten years ago if a school superintendent had sought an "instructional systems designer" for the school system, people might have said, "What's that?" Today, many persons are being prepared to systematically plan audiovisual, library, and computer materials and to use varied instructional methods to achieve specific learning goals—to be "instructional systems designers." The point is that there are a variety of career possibilities open at any one time and the number and kinds of opportunities change.

On the other hand, you don't remain the same either. As you work with children, youth, or adults in educational settings your perceptions and ideas will change about teaching as a career. Some people find that they cannot work effectively with children, that it's hard for them to be with children and still be themselves; some feel they can deal with children but not with the bureaucratic structure of the school. Many feel that they can work with students and with the system, but they think schooling should be reformed. These reactions to career choice are common.

To cope with these reactions you must become aware of your own feelings about the possible consequences of the choices, and try to relate your impressions, feelings and perceptions to the facts or real circumstances. In this way you may reach some greater perspective about relationships between: (1) your talents, desires, aspirations; (2) the realities and opportunities in a specific career (such as teaching); and (3) your personal concept of the good life. Your goal should be to achieve some match between who you are, what you wish to do, and the possible careers in which you may find success and satisfaction.

In other words, do all you can to gain a fuller understanding of (1) who you are as a person; (2) where your talents, capabilities, and shortcomings lie; and (3) the realities of the world of teaching—then you'll be in a much better position to make at least a tentative decision about a career that may fit you. You can then look at yourself as a person and as a future professional against the backdrop of a teaching career and what it takes to be successful and happy in the work of teaching.

The one major reason that many college students have difficulty in making career decisions is that they accept the mistaken view that such decisions should be final. This was never completely true and is being contested more and more as society recognizes that people change, work and leisure and attitudes toward the two change—society and the world are changing. Currently, projections are that those entering the world of work will make as many as four or five major career changes during their lives. To you, this may be reassuring or frightening, or a little of both. Hopefully, it will help you to approach career decision-making with more openness and less anxiety and also help you to be aware of the need for you to be able to adapt to and cope with change.

The Demand for Teachers Today

At almost any time throughout the history of the United States, a person with some higher education or with a college degree could get a job as a teacher. In the past (except during the Great Depression of the 1930's), there has been a shortage of college-educated manpower and this shortage meant a shortage of qualified teachers. (It is interesting to note that in certain teaching fields, for example, high school social studies and male athletics coaching, there has never been a shortage of teachers since the 1920's.)[1] Beginning in 1970, the situation changed quickly. Now we have surpluses of teachers in terms of immediate and traditional school demands, and these surpluses are being felt across the country. The National Education Association, in a recent survey of teacher supply and demand, reported that the job shortage in public school teaching was likely to continue into the early 1980's. Unless drastic changes occur in the number of people completing teacher education programs or in the rate with which school systems use personnel through improvement of programs and staffing, the job shortage will continue. As you consider preparing yourself for a career in teaching you will need to face squarely the supply and demand situation.

What are the causes for the teacher surpluses which seemed to occur almost overnight? Here are some of the major ones: (1) lowered birth rate; (2) greater supply than demand; (3) increased class sizes; and (4) change in government spending.

Birth Rate. The birth rate in the United States has been dropping consistently since 1957 and is now at the lowest level in modern history. School enrollments, of course, are directly related to the birth rate. During the period 1969-1975 the overall school population actually increased slightly, but the elementary school population began a slow, steady decline from 32,010,000 in 1969 to 29,961,000 in 1975. This difference of over two-million children means that there would be 82,000 fewer teaching jobs in elementary schools in 1975 than there were in 1969. Available statistics lead us to conclude that a lowered birth rate has been one of the major causes for the drop in demand for new teachers. Such a reduction in jobs might not be difficult to absorb if there were a corresponding reduction in the number of college graduates prepared to teach. Such has not been the case, however.

Supply and Demand for Teachers. *Supply* refers to new college graduates each year who have prepared for teaching careers and are qualified to become teachers. *Demand* refers to the number of positions available to teachers. The demand for teachers involves two factors: the first is the number of new graduates who seek teaching jobs after graduation (typically, almost one-third of the new graduates do not); the second is the annual turnover of teachers, those who leave teaching or leave the position they held the previous year. Estimates are that there is more than an 8 percent turnover in the faculties of elementary and secondary schools each year. The number of former teachers re-entering service amounts to about 3 percent. The actual number of positions to be filled by new teachers is approximately 5 percent of the total number of teachers in elementary and secondary schools. Since the total estimated teaching force in public and private schools will be approximately 3,000,000, it is estimated that there will be openings for about 150,000 beginning teachers each year during the 1970's.[2] This means that only those with the best qualifications may find jobs.

Increased Class Size. A third factor contributing to an over-supply of teachers is that class size has been increased by school districts in order to save money; this, of course, has reduced the number of teachers employed in many school systems. In the past, most school systems sought to maintain a given pupil-teacher ratio of 25 to 1 or 30 to 1, but a taxpayers' revolt and funding limitations have forced many schools to increase these ratios to 30 or 35 to 1. Actually, if we were financially able to maintain preferred class sizes, the United States probably would not have a surplus of teachers.

Changed Government Spending. Another reason for a growing surplus of teachers has been a change in the way government leaders have felt about spending money for education. Public education had been seen as a good means of maintaining and improving our society because it provided opportunity for the children of the poor or less fortunate, as well as the rich and not so rich. The federal and state governments provided considerable new funds for

4

educational reform efforts in the 1960's, allegedly to help minority groups and the poor to gain access to the economic system. In the early 1970's, however, studies of the impact of the new funds on the opportunities for children and youth raised serious questions.[3] Leaders in the Executive branch of the federal government used these studies as justification for not releasing some congressionally authorized funds for education.

Given fewer dollars from federal sources, along with growing inflation and the reduced worth of the dollar, the press for solving urban problems, loss of confidence in elected political leaders, continuation of outmoded and unequal property taxes—citizens and school boards began to call for a reduction in the number of professional staff employed in schools, throwing hundreds of teachers out of work across the country.

Improving the Demand for Teachers

How can the supply of teachers be decreased or the demand for teachers increased?

It is not that so many fewer new teachers will be employed in future years as it is a situation of overproduction. Some estimates are that the number of teachers who will complete preparation programs during the 1970's will be more than twice the number in the 1950's. Obviously one way to deal with the situation is to reduce the supply of teachers by either limiting the number who are admitted into preparation programs or by reducing the number who are allowed to complete them. Some state legislators have talked about establishing quotas for teacher education students in public colleges and universities; public outrage at limiting career opportunities through legislation has caused the quota idea to be discarded. On the other hand, legislators in some states are reducing appropriations to colleges of education so that colleges have had to reduce their faculties and hence their enrollments.

The situation you face is that you may have to respond to higher admission or selection standards for teacher education as well as the possibility that minimum certification requirements for beginning teachers might be increased. By increasing these requirements the annual

5

production could be reduced from 200,000 new teachers each year to 150,000. Over a ten-year period there would be a half million fewer teachers in the manpower pool.

The outlook for teacher demand is not as gloomy as it may appear at first sight. In a study the National Education (NEA) suggested these possibilities for improving the demand:

- Replace teachers who have had substandard preparation.
- Reduce class size in the elementary schools to 24 and minimize teaching loads of secondary teachers to 124 for the school day.
- Extend kindergarten and nursery school to include the same proportion of preschool-age children as now are enrolled in the primary grades.
- Restore curriculum offerings which have been discontinued because of teacher shortages.
- Develop plans to prevent assignment of teachers to subjects or grades for which they are unprepared.
- Enlarge the coverage of special education programs.
- Fill positions created by normal turnover and enrollment changes.[4]

It may be noted that these are all "external screenings" or "external selection procedures" (done by others to the student, not by the student himself). There is a great deal to be said for self-selection procedures, in which students are given the opportunity to decide initially, for themselves, whether teaching is the career for them. With earlier experiencing of the "real world of teaching," it is possible that many students would choose careers other than teaching.

There still are some fields with teacher shortages and there are new and growing areas of opportunity. These are the areas which seem to be most open at the time of our writing:

- Special education teachers, especially teachers of the physically handicapped and the emotionally disturbed.
- Teachers of children from low income families.
- Teachers of vocational and technical subjects.
- Bilingual teachers.

- Private school teachers.
- Teachers of young children, ages three to eight.

The area of preschool or early education is growing. The education of young children, especially preschool age, is a whole new program yet to be fully developed in most American schools. Only in recent years have both teachers and the public realized that children begin to learn essential material and, indeed, form the means for later learning, below the age of six. This, coupled with the fact that we can create conditions for young children which stimulate their intellectual and physical development so that they can profit from later school and nonschool learning experiences, means that more and more public resources are going to be provided for the education of young children.

Some of this work no doubt will be done with parents in their homes, some in special nursery school facilities in which parents and teachers can share in providing learning experiences for their children. Some colleges and universities are currently offering parent education programs which have a two-fold purpose. These programs assist parents in preparing their children for school, assist teacher education students in learning to work with parents, and, in conjunction with the parents, provide better assistance for the children. In any case, more teachers will be needed who can work effectively with young children and young parents.

These conditions for improving teacher demand appear promising:

- If the decline in school enrollments were to be accompanied by a decrease in the pupil-teacher ratio, the demand for teachers would remain high through the 1970's. In recent years pupil-teacher ratios have been running about 30 to 1 at the elementary school level and 25 to 1 at the secondary school level. If these ratios were reduced (and they should be) to 20 to 1, jobs for thousands of new teachers would be created.

- We know that the number of high school teachers will increase through 1975 and beyond because the declining birth rate will not affect secondary schools before the late 1970's.

- There doubtless will be a great increase in demand for vocational and technical teachers both at the secondary and junior college levels. The U. S. Office of Education has predicted that such staffs will double in the decade of 1965-1975.

• The so-called teacher surplus of the future could probably be absorbed if there would be greater cooperation between the schools hiring teachers and the colleges preparing them. Such cooperation could result in the preparation of teachers according to present as well as future needs.

Characteristics of Teachers

In addition to knowing about the supply and demand situation, you should know something about the general characteristics of teachers and teaching in American schools. Who makes up the teaching staff; what are their personal and professional characteristics?

There continues to be a larger proportion of women than men in teaching. In a survey the NEA found that about two-thirds of the teaching force were women and one-third men.[5] The number of men (and the proportion) has increased significantly in the last decade or so; now more than half of all high school teachers are men.

In another 1970's survey of 1,500 teachers,[6] NEA found that the median age (one-half older, one-half younger) of all teachers was 37 years; of women 38 years; of men 36 years. The median age of elementary teachers was higher then for secondary teachers; 38 years for elementary, and 36 years for secondary. Approximately 88 percent of all teachers were white, 8 percent were black and 4 percent from other racial groups. Regarding marital status, 81 percent of male teachers were married and 67 percent of women teachers were. With regard to teaching experience, the median number of years for all teachers was 11 years; for men 10 years, for women 12 years. The median number of years teachers reported to be in their present position was 8 years. The average size of elementary school classes was 27 pupils; for high school teachers, the average number of pupils was 135 and 5 classes per day.

Ninety-eight percent of all teachers held the bachelor's degree; 30 percent held the master's or higher degree; less than 1 percent held a doctorate.

The average number of hours devoted to teaching duties during the nine to ten months that schools were in session was about 47 hours per week for all teachers, 46 hours for elementary and 48 hours for secondary teachers. About 70 percent of all teachers were graduates of public institutions; about 30 percent graduated from private institutions. Of the total of all public school teachers, 53 percent were employed at the elementary school level and 47 percent at the junior high and senior high school levels.

Teachers performing their first year of service were 9 percent of the total. Fifty-two percent of all teachers had taught in more than one school system; 34 percent had at one time or another left teaching for a period of time.

In reporting the number of free periods teachers had, 19 percent of the high school teachers reported they had no free periods per week, and 75 percent reported they had five or more free periods. The average number of hours spent in required school work per week was 37 hours for all teachers; 36 for elementary teachers and 37 for secondary teachers. The average number of hours per week spent on noncompensated duties was about eight hours for all teachers. Only 6 percent of all teachers reported that they had teacher aides assigned to them; elementary teachers had a slightly higher percentage of aides than did secondary teachers. Nearly 90 percent of all principals were male; approximately 6 percent of these were black.

The length of the school year in average number of days was 181 for all teachers; 9 percent taught less than 176 days and 17 percent taught 184 days or more. The average annual contract salary for all teachers was $10,254; for women $9,787 and for men $10,654.[7]

Nearly 80 percent of all teachers reported affiliation with some church or religious group. Sixty percent reported that they considered themselves politically conservative, while 40 percent reported they were liberal or tended to be liberal. Eighty-two percent of the teachers reported that they had voted in the last general election.

Summary

This chapter has attempted to give you some information about teachers and teaching today. No one knows how long the conditions we have described will continue. There are several possibilities which could make the future supply and demand situation more favorable. Changes could occur in the way public schools are financed so that reliance on local property taxes could be overcome. The federal government could assume a greater share of the cost of schools. State and federal legislatures could expand public education downward by providing educational services to young children ages 3 to 8. Local and state authorities could, if moneys were available, improve the pupil-teacher ratio. Any and all of these possibilities would increase the number of teaching jobs available to prospective teachers.

There will always be a need for sensitive, understanding, fair, competent, curious, well-adjusted, happy adults in all types of work, particularly teaching. One very important determinant in assuring that the teaching world has the opportunity for such people in its ranks is that you begin to evaluate yourself in regard to these and other human qualities and that you assist others in making sound evaluations concerning you and your potential as a teacher. How do you view yourself on the above-mentioned qualities? How do others who know you well view you on these and other personal and professional qualities? How do you view yourself in the process of becoming a teacher?

Notes

1. See Research Division, National Education Association, *Teacher Supply and Demand in Public Schools, 1971* (Washington, D.C.: The Association, 1972), 58 pp. See also *The Education Profession, 1968* (Washington, D.C.: Office of Education, U.S. Department of Health, Education, and Welfare, 1969), Chapter 3.

2. "Supply and Demand for Elementary and Secondary Teachers," *The Education Profession, 1968* (Washington, D.C.: Office of Education, U.S. Department of Health, Education, and Welfare, 1969). For forecasts for 1959-1975, see Part 4. See also Stanley Elam, "A Somber Economic Picture for Teachers," editorial, *The Kappan* (November 1974), p. 170.

3. Christopher Jencks et al., *Inequality: A Reassessment of the Effects of Family and Schooling in America* (New York: Basic Books, 1972).

4. *NEA Research Bulletin*, XLIX, No. 3 (October 1971), p. 74.

5. Research Division, National Education Association, *Estimates of School Statistics, 1971-72*, Research Report 1971-R13 (Washington, D.C.: The Association, 1971).

6. _____, *Status of the American Public-School Teacher, 1970-71*, Research Report 1972-R3 (Washington, D.C.: The Association, 1972).

7. National Education Association, *26th Biennial Salary and Staff Survey of Public-School Professional Personnel, 1972-73* (Washington, D.C.: The Association, 1973), p. 11.

Opportunities and Careers in Education

2

When you think about a career in education, what do you think about? Do you see yourself working as a teacher in a school like the one you attended? Like you have recently visited? Or do you see yourself working in some other educational role: A principal? A recreation director?

How do you view the idea of a career? Are you clear about what you want to do? Do you have a fairly fixed occupational role in mind? Do you know what steps you need to take to get there? Can you or anyone plan in advance that far? In this chapter we want to explore these questions and provide some additional information about career opportunities in education.

Seeing Yourself in a Career in Education

There are people ending their careers who, in retrospect, seem to have been singleminded and clear about one or more of their career goals. Closer inspection of how they achieved what they have, however, probably would reveal that there were a number of decision points along the way. Neat and clear-cut steps to long-range career achievements occur more in fiction than in fact. One can look ahead, plan, carry out the plan, readjust and repeat the process. But most people find it difficult or useless to project career goals more than five years ahead. For example, it may be realistic to say to yourself, "I want to work with little children in informal settings and I'm going to take whatever preparational steps necessary to get there." But it might be more frivolous to say "No matter what happens, I'm going to stay in my hometown and teach second grade." In thinking about a career the wise person probably has broad long-range goals (more than five years), and fairly precise short-range goals (less than one year), recognizing that most career planning decisions are in the intermediate range (one to five years).

Careers in teaching in both public and private schools have been criticized because of their "flatness." This criticism of teaching comes from observations such as: (1) learning to teach skillfully is complex and difficult; (2) beginning teachers have to work very hard to master their subjects organize their materials, develop individually tested teaching techniques which work for them; (3) once teachers know how to teach effectively, they tend to use the same materials and techniques over and over again— they relive each year the same experiences of the year before. Under these circumstances, if accurate, teaching essentially would be routine and maximum career achievement would occur after five to seven years of teaching.

However, there is no reason for teaching to ever become routine—for teaching to become a "flat" career—if proper guidance is provided in career decision-making. Such guidance should assist potential teachers to understand themselves and their own attitudes, to be aware of what constitutes career satisfaction for them, to determine their levels of curiosity and thirst for learning and self-improvement, and to determine their adaptability to change.

A teaching career will never become "flat" for a person who is curious, anxious to learn, and adaptable to change, for such people will build in their own interest and excitement by the type of people they are, or will be intelligent and creative enough to modify their career plans in order to provide the change needed to keep them interested and challenged.

The possibility that a person will "settle into" a situation so that he no longer questions the system or tries to change it is found in all types of work. In public school teaching outside factors may tend to compound the possibility of this occurrence. Some personnel policies and practices tend not to encourage change in location, change in assignment, change

13

in teaching style, or change in intermediate career goals. If the teacher is to maintain a sense of vitality and growth to which students respond, that teacher must be interested and alive to new possibilities, choices, and adventures. The teacher who is trying to stimulate learning in others needs to be a lifelong learner. This means that as time passes a teacher must develop new interests, create new intermediate range objectives, seek new learning opportunities, discard previously organized materials and try new techniques. The teacher needs to be open to the world in which he lives. Such openness allows for, in fact requires, constant growth. Can you identify people in whom openness and a liveness exist? Have some of them been your teachers, and have they stimulated you as a student? How do they compare to others whom you may view as having "settled in?" Can you capture the spirit of openness?

Types of Schools

Suppose your first career goal is to be a good and successful classroom teacher; what options do you have? You could teach in a public or a private school. You could teach in a nursery school, kindergarten, primary school, middle school, junior high, high school, community college, vocational-technical school, adult evening school, college or university. You could teach almost any subject. You could work in special education, with children who are handicapped, deaf, blind, or who are in some other way "exceptional." You could work with persons who have learning disabilities: for example, people who for some reason did not develop adequate reading skills during the primary grades.

In addition to these options, there are many opportunities available within a school either because of the unique goals the faculty is working toward or because of the way teachers and other school personnel work together. More school systems are beginning to realize that programs offered to students in a building should draw upon the unique interests and talents of the principal and staff members in that building. For example, in some schools teachers work in teaching teams; in others teacher aides and volunteer parents

14

are used; some schools allow students to work away from the campus part of the day.

At the same time, many parents feel that school systems should provide alternative programs so that they can send their children to a school which offers the type of program they prefer. Some parents want teachers to stress discipline, others creativity. The idea of different students and different programs offered by different groups of teachers has been catching on. As a result, alternative schools, private schools, instructional "pods"—areas within a school campus—have been established.

The concept, and even the term "alternative school," sometimes also termed the *free school,* is relatively new. Herbert I. Von Haden and Jean Marie King provide this definition: "The free school is an alternative to the public school and is established on the philosophy that a child learns best when he is curious and feels a need to learn. It is an attempt by communities of people to replace the conventional school with a free school—free from authoritarian control of students and their learning, free from courses of study, school regulations, bells, texts, and administrators. Students are allowed to come and go as they please. By placing planning, execution, and evaluation of learning in the hands of the students, the advocates of alternative schools propose to develop enough confidence and responsibility in the students to enable them to handle their own affairs."[1] If you are interested in *becoming a teacher,* but traditional forms of education are not exactly what you're looking for, perhaps you'd be a good "alternative teacher."

Some private schools have been established because parents want special learning environments for their children and they have the wealth and resources to support such efforts. Such schools may be located in the countryside, or in Europe, or may stress particular theories or methods. For instance, the Montessori Method is an approach to educating preschool children, usually between the ages of three and six, through the performance of simple tasks using specially prepared materials and equipment. The Montessori approach may also be used all through the elementary grades. If you are interested in a special type of philosophy, you might wish to investigate means and methods of earning Montessori certification, which requires particular courses and experiences.

From our perspective there are advantages and disadvantages in working in privately supported schools. Some advantages may be: Because many private schools are established for particular purposes, the goals of the teachers, the administration, and the parents usually agree. Many private schools are resident schools; therefore, teachers see their students in all kinds of circumstances and can become involved in the nonacademic life of students. Often the performance expectations for private school teachers are traditional and clear. In such cases, the teacher lectures, gives assignments, hears recitations, marks papers and gives grades, and has very little contact with parents. On the other hand, there are private schools in which the role of the teacher is relatively free and can be created as the teacher works with the students and the parents. In other words, private schools may sometimes offer a wider range of choice for students and teachers than public schools.

Some of the disadvantages of teaching in a private school seem to be these: Because schooling is expensive most private schools are not adequately financed—not as well financed as public schools. Job security, salary, fringe benefits for teachers (insurance, health care, retirement), all are associated with finance. Therefore, one may expect private school teachers to earn less than public school teachers. And, because contracts between a school and a teacher are private, there are great variations in the salaries paid to teachers, in the same school, carrying similar responsibilities. In traditional private schools most decisions are made by the headmaster (principal) without the involvement of the faculty. (For those persons who prefer not to be involved, this could be considered an advantage.) Private school teachers are not as well organized as public school teachers; very seldom do private school teacher organizations participate in collective bargaining or negotiations.

Opportunities in Education

What different roles or jobs are found in the various kinds or levels of schools?

Nursery Schools and Kindergartens. Most schools for young children are comparatively small; therefore, the staff usually consists of one to five teachers and a head teacher or director. In addition you might find these positions on a part-time basis: child development specialist or child psychologist, school nurse, audiologist, speech correctionist, media or audiovisual specialist, home-school liaison person, parent and family-life education or child care specialist. In visiting modern nursery schools you would notice that parents are encouraged to participate in the instructional program.

Elementary Schools. Elementary schools vary in size from one-room schools located in remote rural areas housing five or ten students, to large urban schools enrolling 1,000 or 1,500 youngsters. An average-sized urban or suburban elementary school has a professional staff of 18 to 20 classroom teachers and one principal. Some schools also include the following personnel, at least on a part-time basis: a vice principal; an elementary counselor; a school or child psychologist; special subject teachers who teach art, music, or physical education; a school librarian and media specialist; a special reading teacher; a speech correctionist; a school nurse; a psychometrist (conducts psychological testing); a home-school coordinator and attendance officer; a visiting teacher; a person who coordinates the work of student teachers and organizes inservice programs for the staff. You should note that in most cases, specialists and special teachers have developed their specializations after they have had experience as regular classroom teachers.

Some elementary schools require that the teacher work on a team with other teachers (team teaching). Sometimes these teams are structured, the work of the individual team members being differentiated according to subject or administrative responsibility. For example, a team might be composed of teachers with different subject backgrounds, or members of the team might be given different organizational status and tasks (team leader, regular teacher, assistant teacher).

Some elementary schools are based on an "open school" concept. Instead of being separated by classroom walls, children work in larger spaces, often called "pods," and move to special work areas as they change learning tasks. In a similar way, out-of-school experiences are better coordinated with in-school activities. For example, children may imitate television characters in classroom dramatizations or work on the lines to be used in a backyard play in language arts classes. Teachers who work in these kinds of schools must be able to work in the open; that is, where other teachers and adults can see what is being done. (See Glossary for definition of open schools.)

Middle Schools. In response to the realization that the traditional junior high school pattern doesn't always fit the needs of pre-teenagers, the middle school has emerged. These schools, enrolling children between the ages of 10 to 14, focus their attention on two concerns: (1) this age group's need to explore different interests and activities in order to discover what their personal interests and talents are, and (2) to help correct learning skill deficiencies which have developed in earlier years.

In addition to the same kinds of teachers you would find in elementary schools you might find these specialties in the middle school: teachers of separate subjects, for example, mathematics, language arts, social studies; vocational or occupational specialists; tutors; research and evaluation specialists. (See Glossary for further information on the middle school.)

Junior High Schools. Most junior high schools include grades 7, 8, and 9 and are organized very much like high schools. Because of this, the school day is usually broken into time periods or modules. Students change room locations according to some prearranged class schedule.

Some junior high schools try to block larger time periods for students in the 7th and 8th grades so that they will have fewer different teachers. For example, the same teacher might be teaching both social studies and language arts and, in addition, conducting the homeroom or group guidance function for the same group of students. The positions and roles of teachers and specialists found in the junior high are similar to those found in high schools.

High Schools. Teaching jobs at the high school level may be somewhat different depending upon the size, type and location of the high school. Typically, larger high schools offer a wider variety of courses and hence employ many different kinds of teachers. Most high schools in America are classified as comprehensive high schools because they prepare students for trade, vocational, technical, commercial and academic careers. In some larger cities, however, specialized technical, trade and vocational high schools are established to concentrate both teacher talents and specialized equipment. Most high schools are organized around subject matter specializations; hence, most roles or jobs require people who have specialized subject matter preparation. In small high schools subject specializations are broader than in larger high schools. For example, in a small school the same person might teach world history, American history, geography, and social problems. In the large high school there may be several people who only teach American history.

In addition to a principal, most high schools have one or more vice principals, several counselors, a dean of girls and a dean of boys, teachers in the various subjects, department chairpersons, athletic coaches, music teachers, drama teachers, vocational teachers, librarians, audiovisual specialists, as well as the other specialties found in elementary schools. Teachers in high schools are encouraged to sponsor or chaperon various extracurricular activities such as clubs, social events, contests, athletic events, and charity drives. In some schools, the extracurricular events may seem to be more important to parents and students than the regular academic program.

Although some states and school systems are permitting and encouraging varying academic or vocational programs, most high schools are still heavily influenced by the regional accrediting association (sets standards for schools in a multistate area) and what people believe to be the required courses for entrance into a college or university. As graduation requirements from high school have become more flexible, more consumer-oriented courses have appeared: driver and safety education, income tax calculation, economy buying, marriage and family-life education, to name a few.

Community Colleges and Adult Programs. The growth of community colleges has been phenomenal in the last several years. There are now over 1,000 such colleges in the United States which enroll about two-million students. Usually these colleges offer several programs: (1) a two-year academic program enabling students to remain near home and upon graduation transfer to senior colleges, four-year colleges, or universities; (2) vocational and technical programs according to the needs for personnel in the region, for example, medical technicians for hospitals; (3) adult educational and recreational programs for citizens who either wish to prepare for new employment opportunities, or want to learn a skill, or develop an artistic pursuit just for the joy of it.

It appears that community colleges will continue to grow and expand. Community college positions are usually subject- or job-oriented; the teachers are selected from labor, industry, or from colleges and universities. Most teachers of academic subjects in community colleges have the master's degree or higher. Most states do not require community college teachers to obtain teaching certificates.

Generally speaking, community college teachers receive higher salaries than elementary (nursery school, kindergarten, primary and middle schools) or secondary (junior high and senior high school) teachers.

Colleges and Universities. Positions in colleges and universities are also organized around subjects or academic fields. Teachers at the college level usually receive salaries and privileges in accordance with rank: lecturer, instructor, assistant professor, associate professor, and professor. College teachers normally teach classes 10 to 14 hours per week but they have other responsibilities: serving on committees which govern the programs offered; advising and counseling students; holding conferences and workshops; conducting research; writing for publication; and keeping abreast of new knowledge in the field. Most colleges require teachers to obtain the doctoral degree before they grant the rank of assistant professor.

Enrollments in colleges and universities grew rapidly in the 1960's, but by the middle 1970's enrollments were beginning to decline. It would appear that there will be a slight decline in enrollments in higher education over the next several years.

In addition to the positions found in high schools, colleges and universities typically have the following: a president; several vice presidents; departmental chairmen; deans of colleges; deans of men and women; a business manager; a registrar; and directors of public relations, placement, research, counseling and guidance, building and grounds, athletics.

School District Administration and Supervision. Because public schools are organized into districts there are a number of educational positions associated with the governance or control and development of education at the district level. In a large school district one would find these positions: a superintendent; assistant superintendents; curriculum supervisors (for example, supervisors of science or mathematics programs); business manager;

supervisor of transportation, of school lunch programs; and directors of research, of public relations, of staff development.

State Departments of Education. As electronic data processing systems have been applied to educational planning, more and more of the fiscal decisions about schooling have moved from the district to the state. This shift of financial control has meant that state departments of education have become more powerful, more involved in the decisions affecting schooling. As a consequence, the professional staff of state departments of education have grown considerably since the early 1960's.

In a typical state department you would find a commissioner or superintendent, several assistant superintendents, curriculum coordinators for various school subjects, directors of special interest programs (for example, drug education, ecology, student rights), director of teacher education and certification, director of planning, state fiscal officer, school facilities coordinators, director of transportation, director of the school lunch program, state school safety director, school fire marshall, legal counsel for education, public relations director, liaison with the state board of education, director of office personnel, and many others.

United States Office of Education (USOE). Many of the same kinds of positions found in state education agencies can be found in the U. S. Office of Education which is located in the U. S. Department of Health, Education, and Welfare in Washington, D.C.: commissioner, deputy commissioners, directors of divisions, directors of special programs, subject specialists, international specialists, among others. Whenever Congress passes new educational legislation, new positions are created to administer the federal parts of the law. The USOE is a very large organization with many different and varied educational positions.

National, State, and Local Professional Organizations. As teachers have become more organized and involved both in negotiations, or collective bargaining, and politics, more and more positions have been created and paid for by membership dues.

The National Education Association, with a membership of about 1,500,000, employs about 500 professionals. Each state and territory has its own state association which is affiliated with the NEA. State associations also have professional staffs. Many local associations (usually organized in accordance with school district boundaries) employ their own executive secretaries so that the local organization can carry on an active program.

The American Federation of Teachers (AFT), affiliated with the American Federation of Labor and the Congress of Industrial Organizations (AFL-CIO), is also a major national organization of teachers. In a manner similar to the NEA, the AFT employs professional personnel at both the national and state levels.

It would appear that the two national teacher organizations may merge. If this occurs the new, combined organization may bring about "union shops" in education; that is, teachers who work in public schools may be required to join the professional organization. If this occurs, membership in the professional organizations will expand rapidly. As membership expands so will the number of positions needed to staff the new organization.

Future Opportunities in Education

Possibly the best help we can give you as you consider a career choice is to point up developments on the horizon which may make some choices less inviting, and to point to others which according to indications will grow in demand and appeal. Here are some possibilities:

(1.) There is growing interest in the year-round school. Those who advocate such a change suggest two plans: (1) the school year be divided into four quarters of 12 weeks each, leaving one month for vacation; (2) the year be divided into nine-week segments (45 days) followed by three-week (15 days) vacations after each segment. The year-round school uses the buildings and facilities more efficiently, provides the time teachers need for preparation and inservice training, provides teachers with a year-round salary, and engages children and youth in a wholesome enterprise all year. To those who view a career in teaching attractive because of extended summer vacations, the year-round school may make teaching less desirable. On the other hand, to those who see teaching as a full-time professional job, the year-round school may be very attractive.

(2.) Many people are urging a four-day week. The move by the Congress to place all holidays on Mondays is a step toward making Monday a nonwork day. If this occurs, teachers no doubt will want to move to a four-day week, the fifth day being devoted to teachers' meetings, conferences with parents, and inservice programs.

(3.) Research on child development has led many thoughtful people to suggest that public moneys ought to be spent to greatly increase early childhood educational opportunities, especially for the poor. Among those who advocate public involvement in what traditionally has been the child-rearing domain of parents, there are two general proposals: (1) that nursery school or child care centers be established which combine developmental learning experiences for children, health care, nutrition, and other social welfare services; (2) that parent/school cooperatives be established so that parents can be taught to provide the kinds of educational experiences children need, in effect to make the home a richer educational environment. It appears that both movements eventually may be supported. Many more teachers will be needed who are effective in working with children ages three to six and with their parents both in the home and at the school.

(4.) The press for accountability and school reform will force more attention to individualization and the teaching of basic learning skills (reading, listening, organizing, speaking, writing, speculating) in the elementary school. Parents are insisting that their children achieve in these basic skills at some adequate level, and that the school guarantee satisfactory achievement. We predict that more school time and effort will be devoted to individual achievement requiring many more people in special education, psychometrics (measurement), as well as special teachers of the basic skills.

As most children achieve the basic learning skills in the elementary school, the program offered children and youth beyond the elementary school will become completely elective and much more diverse. Students who have demonstrated that they can use the basic learning skills will be encouraged to participate in real world enterprises, to become part of the productive, creative, responsible world of work. Opportunities to learn a trade, to study a subject intensively until personal interests are fulfilled, to try

23

different jobs, to travel, to study nature, to create, to learn to express emotions in appropriate and satisfying ways, to be able to look into all phases of man's interests and concerns; this is how we view secondary education in the future.

There is some speculation that cognitive learning (knowledge, concepts) and affective learning (feelings, attitudes) occur or are located in different parts of the brain. If this speculation is borne out by future research, school programs at both elementary and secondary levels may be reorganized so that both cognitive and affective curriculums are offered and given equal time. At the present, most school work is directed toward cognitive learning.

Through research we are learning more about child growth, development, and learning all the time. As we learn more about how the school and the home can help children achieve the basic learning skills, and as we learn more about how the school can make learning a joyful experience, we will need people in education who can identify and measure the factors or elements which must be present for success to occur. We will need experts in assessment (measurement), specialists in teaching the basic skills, specialists in working with parents, and specialists in providing wholesome affective experiences. And, of course, we will need people to do research and to teach the specialists in these important areas.

(5.) The realization that the good life involves the cognitive and the affective, as well as the psychomotor (physical dexterity and health), is leading to a new definition of vocational, technical, and career education. All students will be encouraged to develop technical and work skills which not only lead to a vocational or an occupational choice, but also may lead to an avocational interest or a do-it-yourself approach to living.

Because man-machine relationships have changed, students will need to be able to respond to the opportunities and benefits of technology, and to accept the personal investments they will have to make to participate in a technological society or a technology-based career. Teachers who possess and can teach technical subjects and maintain easy liaison with people in labor, industry, and community services will continue to be needed. We believe that secondary students will spend less and less of their time on the school campus, and more in productive work activities.

This means that secondary teachers also will be spending more of their time helping students learn (teaching) away from the school building.

This chapter has attempted to make clear that there are a variety of career opportunities in education for you to pursue—some are traditional, some are very new. Most educational positions, as we have indicated earlier, assume that a person has had successful experience as a classroom teacher. Whether teaching experience is necessary for many educational positions has been questioned by some authorities. You should realize, however, that traditionally, teachers have more confidence in educators who have had actual classroom experience. At this time it would seem advisable to learn to work as a classroom teacher before you begin preparation for other educational roles.

Notes

1. Herbert I. Von Haden and Jean Marie King, *Educational Innovator's Guide* (Worthington, Ohio: Charles A. Jones Publishing Company, 1974), p. 202.

The Work of the Teacher

3

Some sage has written, "The more things change, the more they remain the same." This reflection on life seems apt in discussing with you the work of the teacher.

The education of children and youth has been undergoing profound change throughout the world. This has been so because the world itself has been and is changing so rapidly that new needs and new understandings are necessary. However, though the world is surely a changing world, children and young adults with whom you'll work as a teacher are very much the same *inside, as people,* as children and young adults were many years ago. It can be both helpful and encouraging to keep this in mind.

The environment in which these young people spend their lives is ever-changing, and since education tends to be a reactive rather than an active institution in many respects, people involved in the profession need to be aware of new methods, approaches, and ideas related to education.

Here in the United States old ideas and processes are being discarded almost daily; newer, better, and more relevant ones are being tried. What schooling will be like a decade from now, no one can predict with any degree of accuracy. The only safe prediction is that schools will be different—vastly different.

By the same token, what teachers and teaching will be like will undergo changes as profound. Much of their work will be different and, hopefully, more challenging and exciting. Preparation for this new world of teaching is becoming more rigorous and may, in the future, be of longer duration.

In earlier years, it would have been relatively easy to describe the work of the teacher with accuracy, particularly in the days of the one-room rural school when most parents expected only one function of the teacher: to stand before the class and hear recitations. Much of that is changed now. Few school districts have one-room schools. The country has grown, school districts have become larger and fewer. In the 1930's, for example, there were more than 130,000 school districts in the United States; currently there are only about 17,000. In time they may be reduced to less than 5,000. School districts, aided by bus transportation and population concentrations, have consolidated and grown larger. It appears from recent court decisions that, to achieve full integration, districts may become even larger than they are now, in some instances, several counties may constitute one district.

Understanding Students

Teaching situations differ, schools and school systems differ, but some aspects of teaching will be the same no matter where the teaching occurs. The teacher needs to know and understand students; the teacher needs to know how to adapt courses of study to the students' needs; the teacher needs to understand that students' learning styles differ; and the teacher must be skillful in creating a climate for learning.

The teacher needs to understand how children develop and be able to see how individuals vary from usual growth and development patterns. This means the teacher must be concerned with each child as an individual and also as a member of a group. It is sometimes necessary to establish expectations for a group, but to set expectations that all children are supposed to meet indicates a lack of understanding of human growth and development. Each child is a unique person. Each child needs to be considered as an individual.

In the past, it appeared that educators considered all children of a given age as the same in maturity, intellectual ability, interests, and motivation. We now know that this is not true.

John Gardner, in a letter to the authors, wrote:

> . . . If we ignore individual differences, we end up by treating everybody alike. One danger is that we may not demand enough of our ablest youngsters. But if we toughen up the program and still ignore individual differences, we do an injustice to the less able youngster (who may become a dropout). The only solution is to admit that individuals differ and provide different treatment . . . . Our kind of society calls for maximum development of individual potentialities at all levels.[1]

If you are thinking of becoming a teacher, you will need to learn to observe and identify individual differences as well as people's common needs. All humans have needs in common which are physical, mental, social, and emotional.

Abraham Maslow believed that the key to the development of one's human capacities to the fullest degree is satisfaction of basic needs. These needs, according to Maslow, exist in a ranked sequence, and humans must meet the demands of their lower needs before those of the higher levels can surface. Maslow's hierarchy, from lowest to highest level, includes: physical needs, such as the need for food and water; safety needs, illustrated by the search for surroundings relatively free from threats to life and promoting a sense of security; belonging and love needs, shown by the desire for affectionate, accepting relationships with other persons; esteem needs, seen in the desire to be respected by others for one's accomplishments and in the quest for recognition and prestige. Once a person has successfully learned to handle these needs as they arise, he can concentrate his energies on the search for self-actualization. Self-actualization is a by-product of active commitment of one's talents to causes outside oneself, such as seeking beauty, truth, or justice.[2]

The point of this for you, if you are considering a teaching career, is that you will be a much more effective teacher and of much more help to students if you recognize that there may be students in your classes whose lowest level needs are not satisfied and who, as a result, are unable even to feel safe and secure in the classroom, while others may have their needs met to such a degree that their attention is on acquiring recognition and prestige. To be aware of such differences among students and to attempt to work with students where they *are* is one of the major challenges in *the work of the teacher.*

Differences in School Tasks

The differences in school systems make it difficult, if not impossible, to lay down a blueprint of what a teacher's typical work schedule will be.

The number of different groups (classes) to be taught, for example, will depend on a number of factors. Elementary teachers, as a general rule, remain with their group for most or all of the school day. There are variations of this in many schools: schools that are *nongraded,* schools where the staff is *differentiated* (see Glossary for definitions of these terms). In some elementary schools music, art, and physical education are taught by specialists who move from class to class in one school, or among several schools. These periods taught by special teachers provide time away from children so that the regular elementary teacher may prepare lessons, hold conferences with parents, and engage in staff and self-improvement activities.

In the secondary schools teachers usually have a set schedule of a certain number of different classes each day. Five classes a day, teaching one or two different subjects at more than one grade level, seem to be the typical high school teacher's load. Team teaching and differentiated staffing, along with *paraprofessionals* and *teacher aides,* seem to be more and more common in elementary and secondary schools (see Glossary for definitions of these terms).

There are many factors entering into a teacher's load: the subject, the type of instruction required, the number of children involved, the length of class periods, required administrative or supervisory duties, extra class activities, and counseling duties. In addition, innovations such as educational television, audiovisual equipment, and other electronic aids assist the teacher with classroom presentations but require extra work and skill on the part of the teacher. The cooperative planning required for working in nongraded classrooms and differentiated staffing all enter into the calculation of a given teacher's work load.

Many teachers feel that the size of class is the most important factor in determining load. The hope of most elementary teachers is that class size be reduced from 30 pupils per teacher to around 20 to 22. At the secondary level, the average load seems to be five class periods with a total of 100 to 130 students seen daily. Classes at both the elementary and secondary levels should be reduced so that each student can receive the individual care and attention he requires.

Many people seem to think that a teacher is busy only when in front of the class. The truth is that teachers have many noninstructional duties. In a recent study it was found that the average teacher spent 47 hours per week on school-related responsibilities. Ten of these hours were reported to be outside the times when the teachers and students were together in the school building, such as hours spent correcting papers, preparing lessons, attending meetings, talking with parents. In the study, both elementary and secondary teachers estimated that they spent eight hours per week doing required work for which they were not compensated.[3] Eight hours is equivalent to a full day's work in industry. The work week of the teacher is long—too long.

What a Teacher's Work Includes

Thomas Clayton listed a series of major activities in which teachers engage. He said that the effective teacher:

1. Identifies and explains the expected outcomes of the curriculum and ways to achieve the outcomes.
2. Analyzes the needs of the student and makes decisions about the student's present stage of learning.
3. Specifies the objectives of teaching in the light of activities 1. and 2. above.
4. Selects information and materials and makes decisions about the methods which will be used.
5. Involves the student in activities which lead to learning.
6. Directs and guides the learning activities.

7. Provides situations for using or applying whatever is being learned.
8. Evaluates the outcomes of the process.[4]

Of course this series rarely ever happens in sequential order, and few teachers will be universally successful with every child in every area. The teaching process is hardly ever so neatly organized and executed, but all of these points need to be considered and included in good teaching.

Students' parents hold a variety of expectations. Some expect (or hope for) miracles as the teacher works with their children. Many feel that the teacher is a very important person because the teacher is an instrument for moving children along to their full potentials. Quite often parents' expectations vary depending on social or cultural backgrounds. Some parents may feel that their children are being disadvantaged by the school, that their children are getting inferior teaching and being neglected. The work of the teacher needs to be even-handed and fair; the teacher should show respect and concern for every child for whom he is responsible.

The teacher is in a unique and, at times, a difficult position in working with students. At various times a teacher may be a counselor, confidant, motivator, disciplinarian, resource person, or advisor to students. Knowing the correct or best approach or response to make to a student and a situation is a challenge.

One of the most significant roles is counseling children. No one else, not even a parent, is in such an advantageous position to encourage and reveal the potentials of children. Many times these potentials do not show; they are hidden among students' unrevealed dreams, unspoken ambitions, and vague urges. These are rarely on the surface and must be sensed by faint hints of meaning or action. Moreover, children quite often will talk more freely with teachers than with their parents, especially regarding their intimate hopes and dreams. (It should be noted, however, that closer relationships make revealing oneself more threatening.)

Thus the teacher becomes not only a counselor but a confidant, a role to be cherished and safeguarded. Many children whose hopes, to them, seem ambitious, fear

31

being made a laughing stock by revealing what they really dream of becoming. Was there ever a future musician or writer or researcher or artist who openly discussed his yearnings when first these feelings appeared? Some, of course, but most not.

Of all the things teachers do or are expected to do none is more important, meaningful, or sacred than the obligation to notice or attend to the interests of their students, to sense their hidden urges, to offer suggestions as to how to further them. This includes not only involving them in appropriate activities and curriculums, but also providing the means for self-expression. These obligations require skill and dedication. The skills needed may be acquired during the college years of preparation for teaching or during the beginning years of teaching. The commitment, however, seems to be present or not present by the time a person is in college; commitment evidenced by a greater than usual concern for, interest in, and desire to help human beings grow into good, wise, and happy people—to help them in the process of "becoming."

A teacher with dedication searches for ways of motivating students; finding things for them to do that the teacher knows they can do successfully, and sometimes avoiding tasks which, at the moment, the teacher knows they cannot do. Dedication in teaching means finding an interest of the pupil which will drive him to solve a problem or master a principle that otherwise he would fail to do. The teacher who masters the art of motivating children, not just a few but a roomful, has gone a long way toward success in his work.

The Problem of Discipline. With all the unrest in our society, with problems of integration, racial and intergroup conflicts, and the lack of opportunities for youth to participate in adult society, the problem of discipline has become a concern in almost every school and classroom. The old *in loco parentis* (replacing a parent) principle that dominated the American public school until about 1960 has given way to a redefinition of the rights of students; rights such as preventing the school from making unimportant and changeable dress and hair regulations. There is no question that over the past eight to ten years the number of disruptions caused by intergroup or interracial disturbances, the number of assaults on teachers, the number of robberies at school, the number of reported cases of narcotics offenses have increased dramatically. These are the ugly facts of life in many junior and senior high schools today, whether in the central area of the city or in the suburbs. The problems found in the larger adult society are always present in the modern high school.

As schools are organized and run today, principals and teachers are expected to enforce acceptable standards of behavior. This means that a code of conduct, a system of justice, and means for distributing rewards and punishments need to be established in each school. It means that the teacher must be able to spot developing problems, analyze probable causes for misbehavior, move in on the situation with a positive course of action, and keep appropriate records or notes so that the system of justice can operate on the basis of evidence. Many teachers quit the profession because they cannot cope with discipline problems.

Spotting potential discipline problem incidents requires a great deal of finesse on the part of the teacher. One anecdote will illustrate this: A principal and a distinguished guest visited a classroom. It was a cold day, but within a few minutes of their arrival, the teacher said to a student, "Johnny, will you please open a window?" After the visitors left the room, the guest said to the principal, "What was the sense of that teacher asking Johnny to open a window?" The principal replied, "The teacher knew that a window didn't need to be opened, but she knew that Johnny needed to open a window." In other words, the teacher was sensitive to Johnny and his physical restlessness and had given him something to do which provided both activity and recognition.

It is a tragedy that discipline is such a nagging problem for teachers. One cause of discipline problems may be the distaste students have for the courses they are required to take in school. Many times, students do not like courses, difficult or easy, because they can see no sense in them, or because the problems presented by the teacher or the curriculum ignore the peculiar backgrounds of the group or individual.[5]

Discovering appropriate means of responding to variations in the learning styles of students is a common concern for new teachers. Some students have the ability to learn through theory, others must have concrete reality —the opportunity of seeing, hearing, and touching something under discussion. The alert teacher soon learns that students vary considerably in the amount of time they can focus their attention on any particular activity or task; the teacher soon discovers how to shift activity and attention to something else for those with short attention spans.

The alert teacher sees to it that the learning environment is favorable; lighting, temperature, and ventilation are important. The classroom should be comfortable and attractive so that in every way possible it is geared appropriately to the grade and/or subject to be taught. There should be areas of the room planned to attract different interests: libraries, science centers, audiovisual materials, areas with charts, graphs, and posters. And wherever possible, these things should be planned with the participation of the students. This may not always work, but where it does, it gives students a sense of importance and of belonging. A teacher should remember, as a general rule, that the troublesome student is usually a troubled person—one who lacks a sense of identity, one who needs recognition. The teacher should seek to find positive ways students can satisfy their wants. The alert teacher knows that there are individual differences among children, the teacher will seek ways of serving these differences without embarrassing those who differ or reducing the learning opportunities for others.

There is no question that *the work of the teacher* is important, and that the career decision-making behind it is equally important. Celia Denues says, "Because work, more than anything else, can be a way of life that is challenging, enriching, and fulfilling, it appears almost reckless to give little thought and preparation for choosing wisely. . . . Careless career choice can stifle the individual's joy of living. Self-fulfillment is so cherished in our land that we consider the pursuit of happiness an inalienable right."[6]

Notes

1. John Gardner, personal correspondence.

2. Sidney M. Jourard, *Healthy Personality: An Approach from the Viewpoint of Humanistic Psychology* (New York: Macmillan Publishing Company, 1974), pp. 23-24.

3. See Research Division, National Education Association. *Status of the American Public-School Teacher, 1970-71,* Research Report 1972-R3 (Washington, D.C.: The Association 1972), p. 24.

4. Thomas E. Clayton, *Teaching and Learning* (Englewood Cliffs, N.J.: Prentice Hall, Inc., 1965), p. 13.

5. Johanna S. DeStefano, *Language, Society, and Education: A Profile of Black English* (Worthington, Ohio: Charles A. Jones Publishing Company, 1973).

6. Celia Denues, *Career Perspective: Your Choice of Work* (Worthington, Ohio: Charles A. Jones Publishing Company, 1972), pp. 9-10.

Expectations and Realities in Teaching

4

Every person who chooses to go into teaching quite naturally expects to be successful. But, as with other occupations and professions, there are no guarantees that all who enter will succeed. There always seem to be some people who are unhappy in an occupation and a few who find themselves unsuited for the jobs they have taken.

Why are some people apparently unsuccessful? Have they found teaching different from what they expected? Should teachers and schools be held responsible for what they accomplish or do not accomplish? In this chapter we want to explore possible answers to these questions by dealing with the following topics: (1) realistic expectations, (2) the success of a teacher, (3) the success of a particular school, (4) changes needed in schools, (5) viewing problems as opportunities.

Realistic Expectations in Teaching

We have tried in some of the previous pages to give a clear and fair picture of the job opportunities in teaching for the foreseeable future. We have said that teaching is a complex and sensitive undertaking and that the teacher plays many roles. We have indicated that, at the present time, the supply of teachers exceeds the demand, and that a teaching job may be hard for you to find. There are some other points we want to make about what you might expect if you choose teaching as a career:

• As we have suggested earlier, you can expect a good deal of competition for the jobs which are available. In order to compete successfully, that is, to be seriously considered by a hiring authority, you will need to assume the initiative in trying to get any job that is available, including having a placement file established (in your College's Placement Bureau) which describes your qualifications. Your qualifications are better the more leadership experience you have had with children, youth, or adults. The better your qualifications the better your chances will be for employment. To be sure that you have had an appropriate amount of firsthand leadership experience, you may want to volunteer your time and services to a school, Sunday school, adult group, or agency.

• You will always want to keep aware of any openings in a school or district where you might want to teach. You could take the initiative to meet the principal so that he can get to know you. You probably will need to show that you are really interested in a job if you expect to be considered for it.

• As long as there is an abundant teacher supply, and as long as school boards find it increasingly difficult to increase local revenues, remote rural school districts will probably give preference in employment to newly graduated teachers because they start at a minimum salary. In such districts, teacher morale may be low because of a high turnover in staff. This does mean, however, that there are job opportunities for new teachers. You can expect to find more openings in the rural and remote parts of the country and fewer in the urban and suburban areas.

• After you are employed you will probably find that other staff members and the children and their parents really want to be helpful, especially if you ask them for help. Some new teachers are reluctant to ask the principal or a fellow teacher for advice or assistance; they feel that asking for help is a sign of weakness. On the contrary, remember your own reactions when an admired colleague has asked you for help? Don't you respond by feeling useful and flattered? Remember, it is to everyone's advantage for you to succeed, so don't be afraid to seek help when you need it.

We know there are outstanding people working in every school. As you invest time in getting to know your students and your colleagues as unique individuals, as you help and share experiences with one another, you will begin to feel the warmth and the satisfactions which are associated with successful teaching.

• Don't be surprised when you find teaching hard physical work. Ask any experienced teacher and he will tell you that getting back into the routine of teaching each autumn is difficult. It is common for a teacher to be faced with numerous student concerns, with the need to bring the classes to order, with the confusion of arrangement of materials and facilities, with a great number of interruptions from daylight to dusk. The teaching day flies by and the evening is full of papers to mark, lessons to organize, books to read. By Friday afternoon teachers are physically exhausted. The amount of physical and emotional energy it requires to be dynamic is enormous. As you become a teacher, you will need to budget your time so that you get a sufficient amount of rest and relaxation. It is easy to neglect your health and to become overfatigued. With fatigue the teacher is susceptible to all the diseases of the community—diseases to which he is constantly exposed.

• Soon after you are employed you may be asked to participate in inservice education courses or programs. The term "inservice education" refers to courses or programs offered for teachers and other personnel while they are employed, usually after school, on weekends, or during the summer. Usually, the school system offers incentives to encourage teachers to become involved. Some of these encouragements are in the form of inservice points which are to be collected for pay increases, some in the form of continuing or permanent certification, some in the form of special recognition by the school administration, some in released time for participation.

During your first two years it would probably be wise for you to limit your outside commitments and concentrate on activities which are immediately applicable to your classroom. Your first responsibility is to become a masterful teacher, as described on pages 30 and 31.

Becoming a masterful teacher admittedly is a lifelong enterprise. However, the way you view teaching and the way you organize your own time and talents during your first years of teaching usually become a way of life. It is important, therefore, that you continue to question yourself about how you are spending your energies and your time. You need to ask yourself such questions as these: Am I focusing on trivia when important events are taking place? Am I maintaining a spirit of adventure in my classroom? Are we, my students and I, creating a climate for learning of which we are proud?

• Unless you are superhuman or you slight your own professional development, you will find that teaching is a full-time job. You will be confronted with so many students who need special attention and so many tasks to be done it will be easy for you to become either overextended or to feel guilty about not being able to do more. But you will not be able to be effective unless you can maintain your normal energy level, keep your sense of humor, and be tolerant or understanding of yourself and your shortcomings. One has to learn to pace oneself, to handle stress with graciousness, and to be oneself. You can't be all things to all people.

The Success of a Teacher

The success of an individual teacher is not easily defined. The difficulty in establishing a set of always-applicable standards for judging success is that criteria used have to be related to the time, the circumstances, and the purposes of the particular people involved. We still believe you should be aware that standards for success do exist in the traditions and the customs of schools. Such criteria as the following examples are important to the new teacher because a teacher is more than likely to be judged successful or unsuccessful in relation to them:

(1.) The teacher should maintain an orderly and purposeful classroom. Principals stress and new teachers learn that some form of order, control, or discipline is often essential if the work of the school is to be carried forward.

(2.) The teacher must be consistently honest and fair in dealing with students. Students at all levels observe their teachers carefully; they can spot inappropriate behavior immediately. They also react strongly and negatively to favoritism or injustice. (This is especially true of students at the middle school level and above.) The teacher who explains why he does what he does, who safeguards the individual rights of students, who keeps his personal preferences as *his* likes and avoids making rules based on preferences; these teachers are seen by students as being fair.

(3.) The teacher must be dependable. If a teacher says he will be somewhere or do something at a certain time, or in a certain way, everyone expects him to be there and to do it that way. Although punctuality, neatness, and cleanliness are highly valued, faithfulness and dependability are crucial to keeping an orderly school program.

(4.) The teacher must do his share of the work. If lunchroom duty, playground duty, or hall duty is shared among the teachers, each teacher must do his part or he becomes a burden on someone else. If teachers are expected to greet parents at a special school event or be at a commencement exercise, each teacher needs to take a turn.

(5.) The teacher must be able to work harmoniously with fellow teachers, the principal, the counselors, the nurse, the librarian, the paraprofessionals (see Glossary for definition), the custodians, the lunchroom helpers. The teacher who is sensitive to the problems faced by the other adults who work in the building soon earns their support and friendship.

(6.) The teacher must be sensitive to the public relations aspects of his position. In this regard, the teacher should promote home-school cooperation. Whenever possible teachers and parents should know and understand their mutual goals for the students. Teachers should be understanding and sympathetic in dealing with parents.

(7.) The teacher must be ethical and law-abiding. Teachers may become involved in political activities and may participate in public debates, but parents expect teachers to serve as good models for their children, to uphold the law, and to be ethical in dealing with others.

It is interesting to note that the reason most teachers are dismissed or are asked to resign is because of failure to abide by the criteria listed. Very few teachers have been dismissed because they have failed to teach children specific facts in specific ways. Usually grounds for dismissal are the ones listed: failure to maintain order, unfairness in dealing with students, lack of dependability, unwillingness to do one's share of the work, inability to cooperate with others, inability to deal with parents, failure to abide by the law or a code of ethical conduct. The reasons given for the dismissal of teachers are similar in nature to the grounds for dismissal found in any established organization or institution.

The Success of a School

Many legislators in the various states are asking that teachers and schools be held responsible (accountable) for the money and manpower being spent on education. These legislators apparently feel that if there is a relationship between the amount of money appropriated for schools and the quality of the schooling provided (as many educators have argued), then teachers, if given more resources, should produce more results. Legislators usually define results in terms of student performance, for example, students making higher scores on standardized achievement tests.

We consider such a simple view of the relationships between teaching and student learning unwise and inappropriate. An individual teacher cannot be held solely responsible for the learning achievements of his students. The time the student is under the guidance of the particular teacher is only a very small segment of the student's day. Even during this short time period, the teacher cannot control all the varied influences which affect the student while he is in the classroom. Time at home, time with friends, time watching television, time playing after school, all the experiences of the student influence his learning and ability to answer questions on standardized tests.

If the teacher cannot be held accountable for student learning, what about the school? Can the school as a whole be held responsible for the achievements of the students? We are not yet convinced that schools can be held accountable for student achievement. School personnel can be held accountable, however, for using their resources (for example, personnel, time, materials, facilities) in ways which seem best suited to achieve results, all things considered. The truth is that there is much we do not know about how students learn nor do we know about the relationships between what teachers do (teacher actions) and what students do (student achievement).

On what bases then can the success or the effectiveness of a school be judged? We wish to propose three criteria: (1) Is the school achieving its stated goals? (2) Is the school undergoing change? If so, are the people who are involved in the change questioning their commonly held basic ideas? (3) Are the people who work in the school becoming more diverse, more able to be different? Let us deal with each of these criteria in turn:

(1.) Achieving stated goals. Individual schools usually receive their goals from several sources. Some goals for public education are provided by the state board of education or the legislature, some are prescribed by the local school district board, some are developed by the faculty of the school, some may be created by individual teachers, students, and parents as they interact with one another. Because education is a state responsibility most school goal statements are developed from official documents published by the state education authority.

The statement of educational goals adopted by the Washington State Board of Education is a good example:

Goals for Washington Common Schools

The process of education should . . .

. . . *focus on the learner*

by respecting his uniqueness and individuality.

by providing learning experiences matched to his readiness and learning style.

by increasing his self-direction and decision-making in the selection of learning experiences.

. . . *focus on success*

by assuring learning environments in which each student can succeed.

by helping him perform well and feel good about his performance.

. . . *focus on reality*

by building on the student's need to make sense of his environment.

by extending learning experiences beyond the school building, school day, and school year.

by recognizing that maximum educational opportunity requires the involvement and support of the entire community.

Each student should . . .

. . . *have the basic skills and knowledge necessary to seek information, to present ideas, to listen and to interact with others and to use judgment and*

> *imagination in perceiving and resolving problems.*
>
> . . . *appreciate the wonders of the natural world, man's achievements and failures, his dreams and capabilities.*
>
> . . . *clarify his basic values and develop a commitment to act upon these values within the framework of his rights and responsibilities as a participant in the democratic process.*
>
> . . . *participate in social, political, economic and family activities with the confidence that his actions make a difference.*
>
> . . . *be prepared for his next career step.*
>
> . . . *understand his interests and abilities, the elements of his physical and emotional well-being and be committed to lifelong learning and personal growth.*
>
> . . . *recognize that cultural, ethnic and racial similarities and differences contribute positively to our nation's future and relate effectively with people of all generations and life styles.*[1]

As you will note, this statement of goals is very broad and general but is typical of the kinds of goal statements being developed by states in recent years. Such a statement provides a framework for establishing school district goals and objectives. But how do you suppose one would go about evaluating the schools' efforts to accomplish these goals? Making a fair assessment would require the efforts of many people both in and out of the schools. Although expensive in time and talents such assessments can be and ought to be done periodically in every school.

(2.) Questioning basic ideas. An effective school is one that changes as the community which supports it changes. One way to see if a school is sensitive to change is to examine whether or not the school principal, the teachers, and parents have recently examined the school's mission and goals. Fundamental or important change in the way a school operates usually occurs only after the school's basic ideas are challenged. For example, teachers and parents faced with questions like these may want to change the way their school functions: (a) Should school attendance be required? (b) Are the skills of reading, writing, computing and communicating really being taught? (c) Is the work ethic of our pioneer society still being taught? Should it be? (d) Is our school democratic? (e) Is our school adequately meeting the needs and interests of children? (f) Are our children happy in school? An effective school periodically re-examines the basic ideas under which it operates.

(3.) Individual diversity. An effective institution in a democracy values individual differences and responds in creative ways to differences among individuals and groups. As an institution, such as the family, the church, or the school, persists in time, it should provide more choices and greater freedom for the individual to be unique and different. This means that in an effective school, as it continues, the students, the teachers, and the principal should be permitted and encouraged to play their roles in new and more satisfying ways.

Many people have asked, "How can we tell if we have a good school?" Our response bears repeating. We suggest three criteria for judging school effectiveness: (1) the achievement of stated goals, (2) the reexamination of underlying ideas by those involved, and (3) the development and appreciation of individual diversity over time.

Changes Needed in Schools

When Americans are faced by a national crisis or the consequences that a crisis brings, it is common for them to look to their schools to find a way to respond to or correct the situation. Some social scientists have reported that "faith in education" as a means of social improvement is now being seriously questioned. Our view is that the American people again will look to the public schools to help young people cope with emerging problems and circumstances.

We believe that sooner or later the schools will be asked to deal with national and related international concerns such as (1) attitudes toward and trust of political leaders, (2) energy availability, (3) population, (4) consumer protection, (5) cost of medical and health care, (6) national economy, (7) life goals. There are many others. Can and should the schools take on such concerns? We are uncertain about an answer to this question. Our experience would lead us to say that the schools should *not* take responsibility for these problems, at least not directly. But we also know that the schools can contribute to the solution of these problems and to new problems as they arise, especially if schools can be changed. Schools may be changed so that they can contribute directly to the solution of some of America's major concerns by:

• *Breaking down the distinctions between school and nonschool life.* In a rapidly changing society, living and learning are inseparable. Children, youth, and adults need to be together in doing the work of the society. Separating children from the society, separating children from the world of work reduces their learning opportunities. Not providing schooling for adults is equally shortsighted. Developing opportunities for all people to become increasingly open to new experience and new knowledge, to increase knowledge, to increase awareness, to become responsibly free—these are possible. Getting everyone involved would apply an unlimited amount of human energy for work on common concerns.

• *Making school a resource and retreat center for dealing with human problems.* The school should be a place where people can pursue both individual and group interests, where teachers can assist the progress of rather than control learning. Many and perhaps most of life's lessons can be learned best in the home, the neighborhood, the work site, wherever it is. But the interested and involved person needs periods of rest, renewal, reflection, the exact kinds of activities which can best be carried out in a central facility such as a school building. Schooling should be seen as *part of* living, not *apart from* it.

• *Having the school be a place where individuals clarify and confirm their values; helping people create a sense of community and a responsibility for the common good.* Schooling to meet human needs is collaborative; by collaborative we mean that the whole process from goals to ways to achieve these goals must be planned and undertaken by those who are affected. A person's values become clear as he reflects upon the consequences of choices he has made. A person's education is made greater each time he examines the basic ideas and values on which he makes his choices. It becomes extremely important, therefore, for the school to be a place where people are free to question, to explore, to try out, to make mistakes. It becomes doubly important for the school to be a place where people are cherished, a place where people care about people.

- *Focusing the work of the school on helping children become good self-managers.* A good manager is a person who, conscious of himself, the situation in which he is located, the work to be done, initiates action in keeping with his values. Teachers and administrators in today's schools must realize that education is fundamentally a power-sharing activity, giving or allowing the student to have and take power, so that he can become spiritually independent, can make up his own mind, and can become socially and appropriately interdependent. A good manager has power, power to discipline himself and power to influence others. For schools to be places for the training of managers, there must be opportunity for preparation for management: studying, making choices, trying out ideas, and undergoing the consequences.

If schools were organized as suggested here, would they be very different from what most schools are today? We think the schools we have projected would be very different:

- Parents and children would go to school together.
- After individuals had mastered the basic learning skills (most of these could be mastered at home or in the neighborhood), all schooling would be voluntary and elective.
- All individual evaluation related to the performance of a group would be eliminated. Grading would be unnecessary. Each student would receive individual feedback on those matters about which he requested responses. All other feedback would be directed to the group in relation to the goals and activities the group developed.
- The atmosphere everywhere in the school would be one of trusting, of intellectual and personal honesty, and of forgiving mistakes. Each person would be treated with dignity and respect.
- The school would be the center of community life and recreation.
- Everyone would teach and everyone would learn.
- The professional teacher would have special skills in (1) human relations; (2) helping and problem-solving, helping others to organize for teaching and learning; and (3) educational technology,

skills in gaining access to and using man's accumulated knowledge.

- More time than is currently given would be devoted to sensing beauty, affective learning, and spiritual development.
- The school would be noncompetitive.

Problems or Opportunities?

Looking at teaching from a perspective of the evolution of man and of man's civilization, it is clear that technological change is occurring at a tremendously increasing rate; electronic information storage and retrieval systems, computers, and changes in the whole communications enterprise are causing the nature of education to be questioned and revised. And we know that as rapid change is affecting us, we become discouraged or lost or disheartened; as we see our values being questioned or our jobs being transformed, we often despair. What shall we do? What *can* we do?

Fortunately there are many people who view life optimistically, who recognize the problems and difficulties associated with the world and life, but who view human problems as opportunities for service. We, and most teachers who work with the young, see opportunities for the improvement of mankind as available now as they have ever been. Man finally has the technology so that he can be free. Computers and machines can be the slaves so that fewer humans have to do demeaning work. Computers and machines can do the routine and mechanical; humans can do the creative, the imaginative, the gentle things.

It is useful to consider the ways in which various human beings react to such freedom. Erich Fromm, in his book *Escape From Freedom,* has done extensive research on this idea and raises the question, "Can freedom become a burden, too heavy for man to bear, something he tries to escape from?"[2] Fromm's point is that positive freedom is a result of the spontaneous activity of the total personality. Spontaneous activity is free activity of the self and implies "of one's free will." Activity, according to Fromm, refers to "the quality of creative activity that can operate in one's emotional, intellectual, and senuous experiences and in one's will as well."[3]

Fromm seems to be saying that human beings can only be truly as free as they allow and will themselves to be; that freedom is very much in one's attitude. People who view life optimistically and creatively will probably, in Fromm's terminology, be capable of greater "spontaneous activity" and, therefore, find less need to "escape from freedom."

In his book *The Phenomenon of Man*, Pierre Tielhard de Chardin, after a lifetime of study, sets out the general notion that man is in a long evolutionary process of becoming more and more God-like.[4] He suggests that man, as he becomes more knowledgeable about the nature of the universe and more conscious of his own power, takes on the problems and responsibilities that earlier man might have said came from the gods. Such a view of man in relation to his possibilities is where we are. We think that man is on the threshold of a new day—and the teacher of the future will be in the middle of it all.

Notes

1. Washington State Board of Education, Olympia, Washington, 1971.

2. Erich Fromm, *Escape From Freedom* (New York: Avon Books, 1965), p. 20.

3. *Op. cit.*, pp. 284-285.

4. Pierre Teilhard de Chardin, *The Phenomenon of Man* (New York: Harper, Torchbooks, 1965).

The Teacher
and the Culture of the School

5

One way to find out if you really want to be a teacher is to assume the role of a person who studies society—be an amateur social scientist—and study a school firsthand. We are well aware that you have had more than twelve years of school, that you have both observed and experienced the effects of schools on your own life. In this chapter, however, we are suggesting that you visit and study a school in a different way, with a different set of motives and, hence, with different eyes. We want you to study the culture of a school.[1]

Social scientists define "culture" as learned behavior and results of behavior which are shared and passed on to others in a society. Culture includes nonmaterial items such as ideas, thoughts, feelings, actions, beliefs, as well as material things such as tools, clothing, furniture, buildings. The word "society" may be defined as a localized population which stays together for a period of time in order to accomplish certain ends.[2]

Using these definitions of culture and society it becomes clear that schools exist as a means by which a society shares its culture. Also, a school can be viewed as a small society by itself and this small society may convey a culture of its own. School societies select parts of the culture of the larger society—consciously and unconsciously—and also create their own unique customs as the particular school populations live and work together over time.

It is important as you begin to study the school to be clear about your own motives: your purpose is to learn all you can about a school so that you can decide whether or not you would like to be a teacher. Finding fault with the way institutions work is easy; one can do that in his own family. But remember, your purpose is to study and learn about a school, not to criticize or try to change it.

Your presence and the way you go about your study is important. Teachers are very sensitive about outsiders; they welcome serious students of schooling, but have been "stung" too many times by public critics or reformers who do not take the time to get all the facts about the school situation. The way you conduct yourself and the way you handle the information you collect will reveal your real motives for being in the school.

How then might you go about studying the culture of a school? Here are some suggestions: (1) observe overall characteristics of the school and how the school orders time and space; (2) follow ("shadow") particular people and observe a typical day in their lives at school; (3) notice the patterns of expected behavior, formalities, and rituals; (4) observe and note who speaks to whom about what in the teachers' lounge; (5) analyze your own school experience in trying to study the school; and (6) reflect on what you have observed—internalize it—so that you may determine what it means to you personally and professionally.

Choosing a School to Study

There are a number of different kinds of schools you could study (see Chapter 2). Our recommendation is that you select an elementary school for your first attempt, for several reasons: it has been several years since you were an elementary school student; your perceptions of what occurs there probably will be less colored by recent experience and, therefore, you should be able to be more fair; time, space, and personnel usually are organized more simply in elementary schools; because of class schedules and other considerations, arranging to visit and study an elementary school should be easier.

In any case, there are customs and courtesies you should observe even before you select and enter the school you hope to study. You should first talk with the school principal about what you want to do (the nature of your study), how you propose to do it (methods of study), and what you will do with what you find out (how and to whom you will report your findings). You should be open and honest with the principal about your motives and you probably should offer to share with him any written summary of the findings you may produce.

As you talk with the principal, listen carefully and take notes. The messages he sends will give you many clues to the psychological climate of the school. Remember the questions the principal asks and the suggestions he makes. It may be possible for you to take a portable tape recorder along, but remember to ask for permission to record your conversations before you attempt to do so. If the principal prefers that you do not study his school—this may be said indirectly or directly—it is probably best that you select another school. Usually principals welcome courteous college students who are interested in teaching; they will appreciate your questions and your observations. Because principals and teachers are extremely busy during school hours, try to intrude on that time and schedule as little as possible.

When you are on the school grounds or in the building you will be seen by the children as a teacher and an adult. You should expect to be asked questions about who you are, why you are there, and what you intend to do. After you have been observing in a classroom for a time, you should not be surprised if a child asks you how to do an arithmetic problem or to help him put on his boots. When this happens, you should respond comfortably, referring such requests to the teacher or a teacher aide, explaining to the students as briefly as possible that you are a visitor. Remember you are there to study the school, not participate in it.

Observing Characteristics of the School

What are the things about a school that distinguish it from other organizations? Here are some ideas which might assist you in seeing a school situation:

When you study the school find out what time children leave from home and when they return. In most states the school is legally responsible for children from home-to-home. How long does it take to get to school? How much time does a selected student have from the time he gets to school until school formally begins? What does the student do with his time? What did the student bring with him from home? What did he wear? Do his clothes or the things he has brought with him to school, or the ways he behaves before school starts have any special meanings? What are these meanings?

How long is the school day? Are there breaks? When and how often do they come? Are there stated reasons for the daily schedule?

Look at the school calendar. When does the school year begin? Why does it begin and end when it does? Are there school holidays other than national holidays? When do they occur?

How many adults are there in the school? Are they organized in some fashion? On what basis does the school seem to be organized—according to grades, levels, subject areas, ability groups? Are there ways you can identify a principal from a teacher without knowing beforehand? Do personnel wear visible badges or uniforms?

If you were to describe the work of the school and you couldn't understand the language being spoken by teachers and students, how would you describe the work being done? Do you get a sense of what is considered work on the part of both students and staff?

Make a list of the important words the teacher uses when communicating with students. Classify the words into positive messages (rewards), negative messages (punishments), or neutral messages. Try to note when and for what apparent reasons the teacher sends positive messages. (Positive messages give direction to student action; negative messages stop action.)

Note how often and for what reasons class or teacher activity changes. Note, also, how often and for what reasons outsiders enter the classroom.

Shadowing

One way to get an idea of what life is like for another person is to shadow him for an extended period of time. Shadowing should result in your getting some idea of what a person says and does for a given time period. Shadowing requires the "shadow" to follow and stay with the shadowed person all day, to see and hear whom and what he sees and hears, to listen and watch for reactions, feelings, and meanings. Shadowing provides a look at the relationships which exist between the person studied and his social situation. Shadowing, if recorded, can result in a diagram or a map of persons and social contacts over a period of time.

Given permission, you could shadow a student. This would mean you would have to contact the student, the student's parents, as well as the teachers and the principal. Once you have selected a student for shadowing you will need to arrange your schedule so that you can follow him for an extended period of time. Spending time this way may be very rewarding. For example, if you were to ride home with a student on the school bus, stay overnight at the student's home, and return to school with him the next day, you should gain new insights about in-school and out-of-school activities, especially if the student and his family are of different racial or social and economic situation from your own.

After you have shadowed and taken notes of what you have seen and heard, you may find it interesting to find out what kinds of records the school maintains. Almost all elementary schools have cumulative records: files in which test scores, health records, attendance, teacher comments, and the like are collected and kept. If the school has a guidance counselor you may wish to ask him what kinds of records he keeps. Take note of what kinds of information the school has about your student.

Please remember that shadowing may be an intrusion into the life of another. Such intrusion must not be done without permission; it can be seen as a violation of the person's civil rights.

Shadowing a student will give you some clearer idea of how the teacher and the school culture influence the behavior of the student. Shadowing a teacher will give you similar insight into how the activities of students affect the behavior of the teacher. In some ways, shadowing the teacher may be easier, in other ways more difficult. During the week the teacher usually focuses most of his energies on teaching, one way or another. But you be the reporter on this yourself.

Notice the number and kinds of social contacts the teacher has during the day. Notice the times of irritation, elation, increase in energy, and fatigue. Notice whom the teacher depends on for psychological support and to whom the teacher gives such support. Notice the words or messages which provide comfort or joy and those which cause discomfort or anxiety.

Charles Bidwell, in describing the school as an organization, indicated that the teacher is faced with a difficult situation: being a warm, friendly person and being a strict disciplinarian.[3] The teacher, in attempting to create and maintain student interest, sends messages of encouragement and affection. On the other hand, in order to carry out the responsibilities of the "office," the teacher has to be stern and impartial. Notice how your teacher deals with this dilemma.

Teaching, like all strenuous and demanding occupations, if done well, requires a person to be relaxed and fairly easy-going—to be able to "roll with the punches." Notice how the teacher you shadow relaxes and refreshes himself during the day.

After you have been observing your shadowed teacher for an hour, close your eyes and think about what you have seen. Without further thought, write words on paper as quickly as you can, describing your perceptions and thoughts. Indicate the date and time of your writing and put your notes away to refer to later. Repeat the reflection exercise several times. When you have finished your shadowing you may want to see if you changed the words or language you used in reporting to yourself.

Describing Behaviors

You may find it interesting to discover and describe the way in which school is conducted. In describing the formal aspects of school you may wish to look at the following:

1. Activities associated with the beginning of the school year
   a. district assembly of teachers
   b. before-school teachers' workshop
   c. first parents' meeting

2. The beginning of school each day
   a. call to order
   b. scheduling and assigning tasks
   c. collecting money—for milk, lunch, activity tickets

3. Procedures used for passing along organizational messages
   a. attendance report
   b. school intercom system
   c. reading announcements

4. Ways classroom activities are started and stopped

5. Special Events
   a. holidays
   b. assemblies
   c. fire drills
   d. school carnival
   e. other memorable happenings

   Activities
   a. songs and chants
   b. decorating
   c. entertaining visitors

6. Going to and from different activities
   a. recess
   b. lunch
   c. field trips

7. Events involved with closing the school day
   a. summarization of activities
   b. clean up
   c. announcements
   d. teacher-student communication

8. Events involved with closing the school year
   a. promotion
   b. recognition
   c. social functions

9. Reporting to parents
   a. report cards
   b. parent conferences—personal, phone

10. Procedures for punishment or expulsion
    a. parental notification and involvement
    b. protection of student rights

As you describe a school norm, a pattern of expected behavior, ask yourself why it is the way it is. Are there special meanings to the way things are done? Are they done in familiar ways? Are the patterns of behavior unique to the school or are they fairly established ways of doing things in the larger society?

In many elementary schools the teachers' lounge is a place which is off-limits to the students. In the lounge teachers can smoke, have a cup of coffee, eat a quick snack, mark papers, or do whatever they wish to do during their brief breaks. Observing and listening in the lounge should give you some ideas about what teachers do or say when they are relaxing.

Assuming that you have received permission for your observational study in the teachers' lounge, place yourself so that you will not be in the center of conversational groups. It may be useful for you to have a book and a set of papers to read or sort through as you sit and listen. You should not intrude into teacher conversations, neither should you try to avoid answering direct questions from inquiring teachers. Remember, if you were a teacher, you might be curious about an outsider who seems to be taking notes for no apparent reason.

As adults come and go in the lounge throughout the day, you may want to use some kind of alphabetical code to quickly identify the people in your notes. You may want to use a small notebook and prelabel each page into 10-minute segments. By noting the persons, the direction of conversations, and the topics discussed you should be able to reconstruct the subjects and sequences of activities in the lounge after the school day is over.

Do all teachers "talk shop"—discuss the work in which they are involved—during the time they are in the lounge? Which ones do, which do not? Do teachers complain to one another? If so, about what? What words are used to express positive feelings; which express negative ones? Are conversations easy, strained, confidential, loaded with emotional content? What were your feelings as you listened? Try to record in your notes both your observations (what happened) and your perceptions (your reactions to what happened).

All occupational and professional groups use special language. Professionals use specialized language to communicate particular ideas or subtle shades of meaning normally not expressed by persons outside that profession. Teachers and professors sometimes are seen as either overusing educational jargon or as using language which is not fully and clearly expressed when communicating about professional concerns. You may want to comment on this point after you have examined the information you have collected. You should remember, however, that complex ideas do require the use of special terms; otherwise communication becomes confusing and takes too long.

There are other questions you may want to ask yourself after you have reviewed your data: What were the major concerns these teachers expressed? Did the teachers seem to enjoy what they were doing? Did they like one another? Did they feel they were doing important work?

Again, remember your visit to the teachers' lounge is like viewing a small slice of a much larger school effort. In some ways it is like viewing a person's work on Sunday and assuming what the person does during the week. What goes on in the lounge the day you are there may or may not be typical of (1) what goes on in the lounge on other days; or (2) what teachers talk to one another about outside the lounge.

Reviewing What You Have Learned

If you have followed the suggestions given in this chapter you will have a great deal of information about a school, what goes on inside, who the people are who work there, and how these people respond and react to one another as they go about their tasks during the day. What does the information mean to you, now that you have it all collected? Here are questions you might think about:

- Is the school a good place for people like yourself?
- Is the teacher's role in the school a satisfying one? In what ways?
- Has schooling changed since you were a pupil? In what ways? What hasn't changed?
- What did you like about school when you were a pupil?
- What do you remember about the good teachers you had? Are good teachers the same now as then?
- How differently do you view the role of the teacher when you view it from the teacher's perspective rather than the pupil's?

- How could schooling be made more effective and personally satisfying for the pupil? The teachers? The principal?

We hope your firsthand study of the school has been useful to you in deciding whether or not teaching is an appropriate career for you. You should be cautioned against overgeneralizing from your study, that is, to conclude that what you see in one school is typical of all schools. Some of the things you have seen may be in other schools, but some may not. Schools do have distinctive qualities just as people do.

As you consider a career in teaching we hope you will examine schools and schooling in two ways: (1) as a social scientist, looking at the school objectively as an outsider, and (2) as a teacher, an insider, who shares subjectively in the joys and problems of teaching. Have you been able to view the school both ways?

Notes

1. See John I. Goodlad, M. Frances Klein, and Associates, *Looking Behind the Classroom Door* (Worthington, Ohio: Charles A. Jones Publishing Company, 1974), Appendix.

2. George F. Kneeler, *Educational Anthropology: An Introduction* (New York: John Wiley & Sons, Inc., 1965), p. 4.

3. Charles E. Bidwell, "The School as a Formal Organization," in *Handbook of Organizations,* ed. I. G. March (Chicago: Rand McNally & Company, 1965), p. 991.

The Teacher
and the Community

6

In telling you about the work of the teacher as it relates to the community we need to (1) explain how what the community expects of the teacher has changed and is still changing; (2) report some indications of the status of teachers and teaching according to recent studies; (3) describe how teachers and communities are interdependent; (4) discuss the teacher and the community school idea; and (5) suggest ways teachers might be involved in community affairs.

What the Community Expects of Teachers

As long as the United States was predominantly rural, teachers and other learned persons were held in high esteem by members of the local community. The rural teacher was expected to assume leadership in constructive community activities: to be a church member, take a leading part in church work, teach a Sunday School class, belong to civic clubs, participate in activities useful to society. In addition to being required to live in the community, the teacher was expected to be a model of dignity, observe the unwritten codes of conduct, and in other ways be a wholesome influence on the young. Talk with some older teachers. They will remember their early teaching contracts which forbade social dancing, smoking, drinking, card playing of any kind, being in attendance in places where entertainment was less than socially acceptable by the local church leaders—of being interviewed by members of the school board on these matters.

With the trend toward larger cities in America, with instant and universal communication, with the development of commercial amusement and entertainment, the expectations placed on the teacher changed. Now teachers are not viewed as different from other people; they have all the rights given other educated citizens. To illustrate what the situation is now, let us cite from a recent survey made by the National Education Association:[1]

Only 60 percent of the surveyed teachers lived within the boundaries of the school system in which they were teaching; 78 percent belonged to a church, synagogue, or other formal religious groups; 16 percent belonged to a youth serving group; 19 percent belonged to a women's business or professional, civic-social group; 5 percent belonged to a men's service group; 4 percent belonged to a civil liberties group; 13 percent belonged to a parent-teacher association; and 15 percent reported that they had not lived in the community long enough to belong to a community organization.

Although changes have occurred in the community's expectations of the teacher, especially of the teacher's personal life, the idea still continues that the teacher's lifestyle in a community has a powerful influence on children as a model of proper actions. Children and youth do identify with adults outside the family; the person on whom identification is focused from the child's point of view is a person to be admired, to be imitated, to be like. The teacher is often a nonfamily hero or heroine. Sometimes the beginning teacher is unaware of how much of a model he is to students. It is important for the teacher to respect and be sensitive to the way students view him. As a role model the teacher is a very important and influential person.

The Teacher's Place in the Community

In a recent Gallup poll of attitudes toward education the public was asked to list those aspects of their local public schools they thought were particularly good.[2] The items most often mentioned by the public, in order, were: (1) the curriculum, (2) the teachers, (3) school facilities, (4) activities in addition to the academic courses, and (5) up-to-date teaching methods.

In the same survey people were asked: "In recent years has your overall attitude toward the public schools in your community become more favorable?" Approximately one-third of all the people surveyed indicated their attitudes toward schools had become more favorable, while a little more than a third (36 percent) stated their attitudes had become less favorable (the remainder reported no change or no opinion). With parents who had children in school, however, 42 percent stated their attitudes had become more favorable, and 31 percent, less favorable. A vast majority of public school parents (83 percent) reported that their children were happy about going to school. These same parents (69 percent) stated that schools were better now than when they were students in school.

More than three-fourths of all citizens, according to the same poll, felt that schooling is extremely important to success. With such a widespread faith in education by people from all walks of life, it was apparent that the place or status of the teacher has continued to be important in American communities.

Perhaps one can state strongly that actually the status of teachers can be measured by the size of the salaries paid them. We would argue that this is not the case. Salaries paid to teachers have improved in recent years but they are not close to what they ought to be, especially considering the rise in the cost of living. A growing number of states, either through laws or court decisions, are giving teachers the right to bargain collectively for salaries and working conditions; we mean by this that teachers as a group bargain with the administration or school board to agree upon salaries and working conditions. As the organized teaching profession gains strength through united action, the economic status of teachers may begin to match the social importance of their work in the lives of children and youth.

The Teacher's Stake in the Community

Teachers and parents are interdependent in at least two ways: first, they are both involved and responsible for the upbringing of children and second, they are both concerned about spending local resources for schooling and for education.

Here we want to draw a distinction between education and schooling. By *education* we refer to all the experiences people have in life, through which they learn and grow. Education is lifelong and includes both formal educational experiences—experiences which are planned and institutionalized—and informal ones which may be accidental or incidental. *Schooling* refers to learning experiences provided in the school.

Traditionally parents have been responsible for education, teachers for schooling. It has become more and more apparent as we learn more about child development and learning that much of what we try to do in the school building could better be done elsewhere and vice versa, and that much of education occurs outside the school.

In remote rural America the ties between the parents and the teacher were clear; the parents hired the teacher and the teacher lived with one of the families. Even though times have changed a move to reestablish closeness between parents and teachers is growing in city elementary schools. In some urban schools, parents, to be sure that principals, teachers, and janitors are willing and competent to work with their children, have been given control over who may work in their building.

Some states, with legislators wanting to hold schools and school districts responsible for the funds provided to them, have passed legislation which, in effect, places more responsibility for the achievement of school goals on the principal and teachers in a building. Where this has happened, teachers and principals are required to get local citizen (parent) approval for ideas and plans before they are submitted to the district to be included in the district budget. This requirement for local citizen involvement in planning on the building level has been done, again, for two reasons: (1) to make the public aware of the work of the school, and (2) to create political support by the general public for school operation and hence, financial support.

No other profession is so closely and so broadly involved in the whole community as teaching. Most other professional people, such as doctors, lawyers, dentists, provide services on a fee basis to individuals. Teachers, on the contrary, work with almost all groups in the community; in one way or another their activities touch the lives of most people. Since support of the schools arises from public taxation, each taxpayer has a degree of ownership interest in the schools and their teachers. Too, there is a deep relationship between the work of teachers and almost every aspect of the workings of the community and its progress: its moral standards, its cultural atmosphere, its civic interests, its economic growth, and its vocational and professional occupations.

It is precisely because public school teachers are publicly employed and subject to public opinion that teachers tend to be sensitive to blanket criticisms of schools when national, state, or local crises occur. For example, when the Russians launched Sputnik in 1957, many writers and a large part of the public criticized the schools for not producing enough people trained in physics and mathematics. At the time, no one blamed the federal government for not harnessing the power and resources at its command to beat the Russians into space; they blamed the schools. Yet, within a short time, so aroused was the nation that new laws were passed, massive funds were appropriated, and soon the United States had far surpassed Soviet accomplishments in this field. Because the local school is one institution close to the people and under the community's direct influence, we conclude that this is why it is the first institution people criticize when an emergency or an unpopular trend arises.

There are times when the views of teachers run contrary to views expressed by many parents or citizens. In some communities there are people who believe it is unethical for teachers to comment on social or economic issues, or to participate in political activities, particularly if their views happen to differ from the beliefs of the power groups in the community. Such people express the belief that teachers should avoid controversy and that they should be restricted to teaching the basic fundamentals of learning—what is in the approved textbooks and nothing else. (Sometime you may want to look at back issues of your local newspaper to review instances when teachers were criticized for discussing such subjects as the Viet Nam War, integration, drug abuse, long hair and beards, various forms of school dress, school prayers, and many others.)

But through the years teachers have supported the notion that they should possess academic freedom; they ought to be able to support what they believe to be the truth, and to express ideas considered to lead in the direction of progress for society. The courts have provided a number of decisions which have supported the civil rights of teachers.

Learning from Studying the Community

The teacher, if circumstances encourage it, can use a wealth of resources in the community. Here are typical examples: students visit and study local businesses and industries; students spend part of each day at work with a skilled craftsman; parents spend part of their days at school working as teacher aides and tutors; students canvass the community to determine the views of citizens on matters of community interest; students spend part of each week with older, retired citizens gathering impressions about the past. There are many ways schools can use community resources. Obviously whenever community resources are used by the teacher or the school, the citizens being touched influence the school, the teacher, and the students, and vice versa. Such openness to influence from the outside is one evidence of a good school. Such openness also gains citizen support for schools.

We believe the more freedom teachers have from community restrictions the more obligation they have to become involved in community affairs. This is essential to realistic teaching. It is essential to get the power and energy of youth back of things that any good community should stress. It is the obligation of teachers to help citizens and students of all ages work on the larger human problems: environmental pollution, crime, drug abuse, corruption, ignorance, poverty.

As you may have already guessed, developing and working in a "community school" is neither easy nor simple. Any one school serves many publics (a *public* is defined as a group of people who identify with a special interest, a goal, or a racial or national tradition). In the mid-nineteenth century current varied interests might have been considered a drawback to the work of the school because the school consciously was trying to make everyone alike (the "melting pot" idea). But now, in theory if not in practice, the school values cultural differences. This means that teachers, by the way they work with and relate to students, must appreciate difference and help students learn to do the same with respect to one another.

This involvement of the community in the school and the school in the community means that teachers need to be serious students of their communities. Teachers need to study the social, economic, political, ethnic, and cultural differences found there. They should know about the historical development of the community, its population characteristics, its resources, its religious affiliations, its political power arrangements, its traditions. Only through such knowledge and understanding can teachers and citizens work together to fit the curriculum of the school with the resources and ambitions of the community.

The community school provides a way to mesh the different and legitimate interests and energies of parents, citizens, and students toward the achievement of their common and uncommon goals. The activities the community school can undertake are limitless. General health services is one example: schools could be used for well-baby clinics, inoculation centers, a place for mass physical examinations, nutrition and health instruction, physical conditioning, first-aid training, mental health classes, discussion of public health problems, to name a few. All of the professional and vocational services found in the community could be introduced or partially provided at the school; for example, income tax form completion; an explanation of services provided by architects; family budgeting and banking; information about buying a car, inheritance laws, and business ethics.

Working as a Community Citizen

The teacher, whether working in a community school or a traditional school, is a citizen of the community in his own right. As we indicated at the beginning of this chapter, teachers traditionally have held leadership positions in their communities and rightly so. Over time teachers have become trusted and respected members of their communities and have brought to community service a wealth of skill and know-how.

Here are a few ways a teacher may serve the community:

- As an active citizen. By serving on juries, running for office, participating in political parties, joining and working in civic enterprises.
- As a representative of the teaching profession. By lobbying for educational legislation, visiting school board meetings, working on school levies and bond issues, explaining school problems to parents and students.
- As a skilled human relations person. By observing and giving feedback to groups at work, by explaining needs of children and youth to less informed citizens, by urging increased services for the poor.
- As one who assists parent-student communication. By listening and identifying with the feelings of those parents and students who have problems, by arranging opportunities for open discussions, by being honest and trustworthy.
- As an interested and informed person who enjoys life. By being someone people want to be near.

In summary, your work as a teacher and the effectiveness of the school are permanently tied to the community they serve and from which they get their support. There is a growing need, especially in our urban areas, for schools and communities to come together. For this to occur you must become a student of your community as well as an active participant in it.

Schools just now are re-emphasizing community education. By this we mean that the school should be an instrument for providing needed services to children and their families: to improve health conditions, employment opportunities, and the life of the community it serves. People should be involved in determining the services they need.

Notes

1. "The American Public School Teacher, 1970-71," NEA Research Bulletin. XLIX, No. 4 (Washington, D.C.: The Association, 1971), pp. 99-101.

2. George H. Gallup, "Fifth Annual Gallup Poll of Public Attitudes Toward Education," Phi Delta Kappan, LV, No. 1 (September 1973), pp. 38-51.

Teaching as a Profession

What distinguishes the professions from other occupations? *Ideally:*

- Professions are based upon a body of specialized knowledge, principles, and skills that laymen and members of other professions usually do not have.
- Professions place the welfare of society above the personal interests of members.
- Professions require that members follow a set of principles and values.
- Professions require extensive and continuing general and professional study.
- Professions require a high degree of independence in making decisions with regard to clients and their problems.
- Professions control and protect members so that members may provide high quality service to clients without fear or favor.
- Professions are organized to improve the conditions under which members work and serve.[1]

Given this list of characteristics which distinguish professions from other occupations, what are the basic responsibilities of a profession? In other words, what must a profession do to keep or advance its professional status? Here is our list:

- Define the professional services to be provided.
- Conduct research to improve professional knowledge and procedures.
- Adopt and enforce a code of ethics.
- Recruit talented candidates for the profession.
- Select candidates of high quality.
- Teach candidates to respect the traditions and values of the profession.
- Develop standards for licensing members and recognizing professional standing.
- Accredit professional schools
- Maintain and improve welfare and working conditions.
- Maintain strong and effective professional organizations.

Over the years many people have raised the question, is teaching really a profession? As you take the characteristics and responsibilities of a profession listed above and attempt to describe the current situation of teachers, you may be able to answer this question for yourself.

Areas of Professional Service

The organizations to which most teachers belong, the National Education Association and the American Federation of Teachers, have begun to define "teaching" in terms of job descriptions or activities and in terms of the percentage of time persons devote to "teaching" during the work week. Although these definitions are not yet hard and fast, the organizations generally do agree that teachers are professional workers who hold a teaching certificate or hold academic rank, who spend half or more of their time each day working with students in instructional activities, and are people who do not supervise or rate other teachers. The definition of teachers excludes superintendents, principals, school nurses, counselors, part-time teachers and teacher aides.

It may be only a matter of time before the flow of events and the classroom teachers will force the merger of the NEA and the AFT. If this happens, classroom teachers will be not only the largest professional organization in America but also one of the potentially most powerful political lobbies in Washington, D. C., and the various state capitols.

Educational Research

Teaching has been done for so many years one might think that there would be a great deal of scientific knowledge about teaching. Such is not the case. Teaching is complex and dynamic; that is, many things happen in a classroom at the same time and what happens changes rapidly. It is difficult, therefore, for the scientist, who prefers a controlled laboratory setting, to study an active and alive classroom in operation. And, although the scientist can see what the teacher is doing and can record the teacher on film or video-tape, no one can see learning taking place. Learning must always be inferred from what students do.

Because research on teaching and learning is so complex and difficult, our level of scientific knowledge about the relationships between teaching and learning remains quite primitive. Even so, more research on education has been done in the last 15 years than all the previous years of recorded history combined. Increased federal funds and the development of computers should make teaching much more scientific. But research takes time and is very costly. The National Institute for Education (NIE) was established in the U.S. Office of Education in 1972 and has not received large funding. It will be several years before we know if this agency will be effective in increasing our scientific knowledge of teaching and learning.

A Code of Professional Ethics

There are at least three ways to establish a code of ethics and make it work: (1) a professional organization can write and adopt a code requiring all members to adhere to it, (2) a selected group within the profession can develop interpretations of the meanings of the code and enforce them, and (3) teachers being tried for violations of ethical practices may be judged in the courts, thus creating a body of judicial opinion which may form the basis for a code of ethics. It is relatively easy to write and adopt a code of ethics, but it is very difficult to enforce it. A code is difficult to enforce because an organization seeking more members finds the trial and expulsion of a member to be distasteful and ruinous to group morale. As a consequence, it is difficult to find many cases in which members of a professional teacher organization have taken action to remove a teacher from membership as a result of investigation by a teacher ethics or professional practices committee.

Until 1963, there were many codes of ethics. Almost every professional association of teachers had developed its own code. In 1963, the NEA Ethics Committee, after several years of cooperative study among these associations, agreed on one code called "The Code of Ethics of the Teaching Profession." This code has now been adopted by the NEA and all of the state education associations. Currently, means have been provided through the NEA Ethics Committee for developing interpretations of the code, for hearing cases involving possible violations, and for expelling from membership those teachers found guilty of such violations. Each person admitted to NEA membership or membership in any of its affiliates must agree to abide by the Code, in the following language: "We acknowledge the magnitude of the profession we have chosen and engage ourselves, individually and collectively, to judge our colleagues and to be judged by them in accordance with the applicable provisions of this code."

A booklet containing the basic principles of the Code and the interpretations of the meaning of each as applied to specific cases may be obtained from the NEA.

In the long run, the development of legal guidelines with respect to professional ethics and practices may be the best way to handle legal considerations. After all, if a teacher is accused of violating an ethical code and is to be expelled from his professional group, he has the right to move the disagreement to a superior court.

At the present time professional associations and unions work very hard to protect the civil and professional rights of teachers—as well they should. The staffs of professional associations and unions are asked to provide counsel and help in many ethics violation cases each year. Usually ethics violation cases are handled quietly to protect the individual's rights and the general welfare of teachers.

Recruitment of Qualified Teachers

Far-sighted professional leaders encourage talented people to come into their ranks. Leaders in the field of education have an excellent opportunity for recruitment. They work with practically all the young people of the nation; they could begin to identify talented and promising people, establish a program of recruitment which would be effective, and, most important of all, provide these young people with the support, encouragement, experience, and learning needed to succeed in becoming a teacher.

The teaching profession has not yet organized a carefully planned recruitment program. Future Teacher Associations (FTA) and clubs are formed in many high schools and Student National Education Association (SNEA) groups are found in colleges and universities which prepare teachers. Both FTA's and SNEA's, however, generally exist to provide students already interested in teaching as a career opportunities to organize themselves and to share in learning more about the profession; these student associations have not been used extensively for recruitment or selection.

A few high school faculties encourage promising seniors who have completed their high school graduation requirements to participate as teacher aides in elementary schools part of each day. Where this is done, both the schools and the high school students seem to benefit.

Part of the reason why more recruitment for teaching has not been done is that most teachers feel that students in school should be given a wide range of choice with regard to career. Teachers feel that during the formative years, they should not try to influence students one way or another about career choices except to give them more information about the possible choices.

Also part of the reason why recruitment into teaching has not been organized is that, at this point in time, research has not identified clear definitions of "effective teaching." We do know that there are many different teaching models; for example, that some teachers are more direct and some more indirect in their work with students. We also know that some objectives or goals for teaching some subjects are more objective and concrete while others are more subjective and abstract. Some studies seem to indicate that certain teaching models and some teaching styles or personalities seem to better fit certain teaching goals than others. But we do not know enough, at this time, to be very precise about who should be recruited to be a teacher and who should not.

Some clues to what is needed for effective teaching may be gained, however, by considering results of -opinion surveys regarding "Best Liked Teacher" and "Most Helpful Teacher." In the former survey, done by Hart, 3,725 high school seniors most frequently cited these four characteristics of a well-liked teacher: (1) Is helpful in schoolwork, explains lessons and assignments clearly and thoroughly, and uses examples in teaching; (2) Is cheerful, happy, good-natured, jolly, has sense of humor and can take a joke; (3) Is human, friendly, companionable, "one of us"; (4) Is interested in and understands pupils.[2]

In the latter survey, by Witty, the top ranking traits of the helpful teacher were: (1) cooperative, democratic attitudes; (2) kindliness and consideration for the individual; (3) patience; (4) wide interests; (5) personal appearance and pleasant manner; (6) fairness and impartiality; (7) sense of humor; (8) good disposition and consistent behavior; (9) interest in pupils' problems; (10) flexibility; (11) use of recognition and praise; (12) unusual proficiency in teaching a particular subject.[3]

Several other studies concerning teachers liked by students are given in a text by Don Hamachek.[4] If there is a relationship between teachers who are liked by students or who are considered to be helpful by them and "effective teachers," perhaps we know more about recruitment into the teaching profession than we thought—perhaps we ought to be actively recruiting young men and women who demonstrate such characteristics as those above in their personal and preprofessional lives.

Selection of Qualified Teachers

Selection of persons qualified to enter a profession may take place through one means at one point in time, such as a personal interview or a review of credentials, or it may take place through a series of screening processes or activities. In the medical profession, a great deal of importance is placed on admission to the medical school. Only a small number of openings are available for students interested in medicine, only a small number of institutions have approved and accredited medical schools; thus the entrance process is the big hurdle. Admission standards are often so selective that once admitted into medical school it is not difficult for the student to be successful, although a state examination provided by the medical profession must be passed. The student interested in practicing law, on the other hand, finds that entry into a law school is not so difficult, but being successful in the school may be very difficult. The law student, even if he passes the courses, may not pass the state bar examinations and hence, may not be able to practice.

Traditionally, admission or selection into teacher education has not been difficult. Most colleges indicate that they have standards for admission to teacher education, but when these are examined, the standards are so general that above-average students in any field of study can meet them. Typical requirements include: completion of two years of college, a grade point average of C+ (2.5 on a 4 point scale), good health, and good character.

A large number of teacher educators, if asked, might indicate that they preferred selective retention in teacher education to selective admission. These educators believe that because we do not have a research base for recruitment and selection in advance of teacher preparation, the only feasible way to deal with selection is to let candidates begin preparing for teaching and screen out those who do not work effectively with students at a later time. Some educators assert that selection cannot occur until the candidate has considerable work in the field—work with students in the real world of the schoolroom.

Of course, requirements can be established for admission to teacher education which call for the candidate to make a certain score on a general achievement or an intelligence test. Intellectual ability, however, is only one of several qualities the competent teacher needs.

At the present time, student teaching in most cases serves as the means for checking whether or not a candidate can work successfully in school settings. Usually if a student maintains a satisfactory grade point average and receives a satisfactory student teaching report, he is recommended for initial or beginning teacher certification. Opportunities such as early experiencing programs may change this situation to some extent. (See the Glossary for definitions of Student Teaching and Early Experiencing programs.)

Continuing Teacher Education

Although classroom teachers and the organizations which represent them have a real stake in the way new teachers are introduced into teaching, little has been done in an organized way to acquaint new teachers with the customs and traditions of the profession. Some colleges and universities invite representatives of professional organizations to meet with teacher candidates so that priorities and needs of teachers can be discussed. Some professional organizations, in cooperation with the school district administrators, provide an orientation for new teachers before the opening of school. Usually, however, most information is given informally by the principal and other staff members who work closely with the new person. Many school districts have found it necessary to provide extensive inservice teacher education programs (see Glossary for definition) for new teachers, especially if the district has adopted a particular method of teaching.

It appears to us that professional organizations are entering a new era with respect to inservice teacher education and staff development. Some states are considering teacher centers—organizational arrangements which provide inservice education to classroom teachers and which are so governed that teachers have a major voice in deciding the nature of the experience and the opportunities offered.[5] In other words, teachers themselves, not college professors, do the instructing in these centers. Inservice education may soon be part of the overall bargaining agreement between local school boards and the local teacher organization.

Licensing Teachers

Issuing licenses to teachers generally is under the control of the state board or the state department of education.

Representatives of teacher organizations feel that the teaching profession cannot be held responsible for the actions of members unless and until the profession has control over licensing and accreditation (see Glossary for definition). The NEA for more than twenty-five years, consistently has worked for higher standards in the preparation and certification of teachers. Some states have responded favorably to the NEA's efforts; other states have delayed or have been slow to move.

Most states, in one way or another, have recognized the need for having teachers on the advisory committees and councils which deal with preparing teachers and licensing them. Only one state, Oregon, has given the authority to license teachers to a board of teachers recommended by the organized profession; this occurred in 1973. A few states have all-teacher boards which recommend the standards to be required for certificates. By contrast, most states delegate licensure for doctors, lawyers, architects, and other professionals to boards made up of members of their own professions. (See also Chapter 8.)

Standards for Professional Schools

Accreditation is a process of reviewing all aspects of a preparation program to see if the program meets standards of quality outlined by an established accrediting agency. If an institution is accepted by a reputable accrediting agency, other institutions and the general public have some confidence that persons who take courses at the institution will receive good instruction. Graduates from accredited institutions can transfer their course credits to other institutions without question.

There are several problems in accreditation which have not been fully resolved. (1) Who should accredit teacher education programs? (2) How can accreditation eliminate the certification problems teachers now face when they move to another state? (3) What standards should be used in accrediting programs?

Here it may be sufficient to say that accreditation in teacher education generally is done by or through (1) regional associations of institutions (there are six in the United States), such as the Northwest Association of Secondary and

Higher Schools; (2) the National Council for Accreditation in Teacher Education (NCATE), a group primarily sponsored by the American Association of Colleges for Teacher Education (AACTE), but which was founded by a partnership of NEA, AACTE, and state departments of education; (3) state departments of education. The first group is made up mainly of college and university presidents, the second group by deans of colleges of education, and the third group by personnel in state education agencies. In the mid-1960's, the organized teaching profession had little control of or involvement in accreditation activities, but there are signs that the profession will re-enter the partnership as an active and powerful partner. In fact, it did so in the summer of 1974.

The Teacher and Professional Organizations

As soon as you accept your first teaching job, you will be invited, indeed urged, to join one or more professional organizations. But before you make any decisions about joining one or another you may want to consider these two questions: (1) What kinds of professional organizations are there? and (2) What advantages or disadvantages are there for me if I join or don't join one or more of them?

There are two major types of professional organizations for teachers, (1) general and (2) special interest. Teachers' organizations may also be classified geographically—local, state, regional, national, within the general or special interest groups.

The general organizations, The National Education Association (NEA) and the American Federation of Teachers (AFT), have national, state, and local units. These general organizations enlist member from all levels of teaching, from early childhood through the university, and from all subject matter interests.

The special interest organizations, as their name implies, bring together subject, level, or job-alike interests. The general organizations focus on the common concerns of all teachers; the special interest organizations focus on the concerns of teachers who teach particular subjects or groups. For example, because those who teach physically handicapped children have special teaching problems, they often organize in a geographical region to share knowledge and experience.

Teacher Organizations

Although the present goals of the NEA and the AFT are somewhat similar, their historical roots have been very different. Since it is difficult for organizations to change rapidly, it may be important for you to know something about the historical development of these two groups.

The first formal organization of teachers in America was the Society of the Associated Teachers of New York City which was founded in 1794. Three other early organizations should be mentioned: the American Institute of Instruction in 1830; the College of Professional Teachers affiliated with the Western Literary Institute in 1831; and the Association for the Advancement of Education, founded in 1849. These three were academic in nature and existed to improve the curriculum in education and teaching.

State associations of teachers began forming in 1840, the teachers in Alabama being the first to charter. By 1857, the year that the National Teacher's Association (now the NEA) began, 20 states had organized into statewide groups. The National Teacher's Association was organized at the request of ten state education association presidents (presidents from New York, Massachusetts, Missouri, New Hampshire, Indiana, Pennsylvania, Vermont, Iowa, Wisconsin, and Illinois).

The National Teacher's Association became the National Education Association in 1870 by joining with the National Association of School Administrators (now the American Association of School Administrators) and the American Normal School Association (now the American Association of Colleges for Teacher Education). In 1906 the NEA became the National Education Association of the United States as a result of the passage of a congressional charter. Thus the NEA over the years became the largest and most dominant general professional organization, representing both the interests of classroom teachers and school and district administrators. Only very recently have the administrator organizations left the NEA so that now classroom teachers control internal policies. 1975 membership of NEA was over 1,500,000.

The AFT was organized in 1916, nearly 60 years after the NEA. The national organization resulted from the efforts of some 20 local unions affiliated with the American Federation of Labor, originating with three large locals in the city of Chicago. The AFT, because it was and is a labor union, has maintained its close association with organized labor throughout its history. Labor union policy will not allow management personnel to be in the same union with persons whom they supervise or rate; the AFT teacher union membership, therefore, does not now include school administrators, but until about 1957 it did. Present membership of AFT is about 400,000.

Because of the common interests of these two general organizations many efforts are now under way for merger. Such a merger could have many benefits: (1) the energies now being used to compete with one another could be directed to the teacher's and the public's general welfare, for example, tax reform, the improvement of educational services; (2) the combined membership, when organized politically, could be one of the most influential political action groups in the nation; (3) with political power the status and the conditions under which pupils and teachers work could be dramatically improved.

In our opinion, merger may eventually occur. There are many problems to be resolved, however, before merger can be realized: the internal organization of the AFT is very different from the NEA. The AFT values its affiliation with organized labor for good reason; organized labor alone among major national special interest groups consistently has supported free public education for all children. Both organizations have their own professional staffs; the jobs of these people would be changed in a merger. Both organizations own buildings, have insurance programs, offer specialized services; the legal problems which happen as a result of merger seem almost insurmountable. But merger is going forward. For example, the organizations in the state of New York merged into the New York State United Teachers in 1971. This new organization can speak with a united voice for classroom teachers at the elementary school level, the secondary school level, and at the college and university level.

Special Interest Organizations

If you were to look at a directory of educational associations, organizations, and societies you might be surprised to learn that there are more than 1,500 different groups listed. Many of these are not directly associated with classroom teaching in public and private schools, but many of them are. You can usually find a group organized at the state or national levels with which you can identify no matter what your teaching assignment is.

Some organizations are formed around the age level of the students being taught; an example is the Association for Childhood Education International whose interests focus primarily on children ages 3-12. Many organizations relate to subject matter such as the American Industrial Arts Association, the National Science Teachers' Association, the National Council for Social Studies, the National Council of Teachers of Mathematics, the National Council of Teachers of English. Several organizations are formed by groups that have similar jobs such as the Association of Teacher Educators, the Association for Supervision and Curriculum Development, the Elementary Principals' Association.

Usually national special interest organizations hold conferences and workshops for members which provide opportunities for participants to hear about new developments in their special fields and to share concerns and ideas among themselves. Special interest groups also publish periodic magazines, newsletters, and manuscripts designed to keep members up to date on developments in their fields. Visit the periodical room of your library and look at the number of different magazines published about education. As you pick up a professional journal look to see whether or not the publication is sponsored by a professional organization; most of them are.

The Strength of Teacher Organizations

As teacher organizations have become more independent and able to take firm stands in the negotiation of agreements and contracts, teachers also have begun to have political power. Political power, however, has not come about automatically. It has come through teacher involvement in the political process: working at the local level to elect persons friendly to education, supporting candidates who support education, keeping legislators informed of grass-root political concerns, working to influence legislators in the state and national capitols, and running for political office. A major feature of a strong organization is that it is actually involved in the affairs of the community, state, and nation. It makes its views known and its influence felt on all levels of government.

Another feature of a strong organization is that it protects its members from unfair attack and defends them, if necessary, in the courts. It is not uncommon for a teacher to be fired without due process, that is, without being advised of charges which have been made against him, to have a hearing, to face his accusers, to call witnesses in his own behalf; in other words to be fired in a manner inconsistent with his constitutional rights. When this occurs, it is very important for the teacher to have an organizational base from which he can receive legal advice and assistance. Because court trials are so expensive, it is almost impossible for the individual teacher to defend himself. Both the AFT and the NEA have special funds set aside for the defense of their members.

A third feature of a strong organization is that it is responsive to its members and their needs. (For example, if the elementary school teachers needed a short break during the morning hours, the responsive organization would work with the school board and administrators to have the daily schedule changed.) This means that the organization should be simple in its structure and that it should employ staff personnel who are effective and efficient in carrying out the goals of the organization.

Should I Join?

What benefits can a person expect from belonging to an organization? Why join anyway? There are teachers who do not join any organization. If you were to ask them why, they might give these reasons:

- Organizational dues are expensive. "My beginning salary is low and I still have debts from college; I simply can't afford it."
- Time is scarce and participation takes time. "I would join but there is no sense in my paying dues unless I have the time to be involved in the organization."
- The organization's program is inadequate. "I would join but meetings are not worthwhile and I don't agree with what the leaders in the organization are doing."
- People hesitate to be committed to organizations or causes. "People are after you all the time to do this or that; frankly, I don't want to be involved in an organization."

Some reasons that you might consider for joining one or more professional organizations are:

- A professional worker is concerned for his own personal welfare as well as the welfare of all who work in the schools.
- In a complex society a person does not have much political power—power to influence how resources are shared and spent—without membership in an organization which supports his interests. In other words, to have a voice which is loud enough to be heard, one needs to join with similar voices.
- The teacher's ultimate psychological and legal support in improving or changing the way the school operates will come from colleagues and organizations to which he belongs. Almost every school district has some record of a teacher who might have been dismissed or harassed if a professional organization had not been ready to provide technical and financial help.
- Professional organizations influence policy-making at the school board or district level, at the state board of education and state legislative levels, and at the U. S. Office of Education and national congressional levels. Professional organization representatives watch governmental opera-

tions at all levels; they give testimony to legislative committees; they write and have introduced special educational legislation.

- Professional organizations provide special group services. Teachers are good financial risks; as a consequence, members of teacher organizations can enjoy special life and health insurance, special investment plans, group buying discounts, special holiday travel arrangements. As teacher organizations become more powerful, they will be able to operate their own financial services.

- Professional organizations provide a means for professional workers to keep up with new developments in their field, to find out about research and development, to hear from other professionals who face the same problems that they face.

- Professional organizations provide an opportunity for service—to be identified with a group and a cause—to have a way to do something concrete to improve schooling and teaching and to increase the knowledge we have of the teaching process.

This chapter has focused on teaching as a profession, on how teachers currently are organized, and on how and why teachers join general or specialized organizations. As you reflect on what you have read you may wish to respond to these questions:

- What are the characteristics and responsibilities of a profession?
- How are teachers recruited, selected, prepared and certified? Who controls these processes?
- How are the colleges which prepare teachers approved?
- Is teaching really a profession?
- How have the NEA and AFT organizations developed?
- Do you think you will join a professional organization if and when you become a teacher?

Notes

1. T. M. Stinnett, *Professional Problems of Teachers.* (New York: The Macmillan Company, 1968), pp. 55-70. See also Morris L. Cogan, "Toward a Definition of a Profession," *Harvard Education Review* (Winter 1953), 23: 33-58.

2. F. W. Hart, *Teachers and Teaching.* (New York: The Macmillan Company, 1934), pp. 131-132, 250-251.

3. P. Witty, "An Analysis of the Personality Traits of the Effective Teacher," *Journal of Educational Research,* 1947, 40:662-671.

4. Don Hamachek, *Encounters with the Self* (New York: Holt, Rinehart & Winston, 1971), pp. 195-196.

5. See Teacher Education Center Act of 1973, State of Florida, Tallahassee, Florida.

Legal Requirements
for Teachers

8

If you want to teach in public schools you will need to get a certificate. As is true of nearly all professions, licensing by the state is required to enter and continue in professional service. Obtaining a license or certificate is required for all teachers in the public schools. Requirements for teaching in nonpublic schools vary from state to state as we shall see below. In all states, the authority for issuing teacher certificates is currently in the hands of the state department or board of education.

There are good reasons for such requirements. First, children and youth must be safeguarded against the unqualified. Second, there must be a guarantee that professional personnel can provide high quality service to the public; otherwise the public's money, either taxes or fee payments, will be wasted. And third, the competent person who has spent years preparing for service in a given profession requires protection against the unqualified.

A History of Licensing Teachers

Licensing of teachers (although *licensing* and *certification* are not exactly the same, the terms are used interchangeably here) in the United States began in a rather haphazard manner. During the colonial period, schools sprang up in local communities with no state help or controls. They were subscription schools, that is, parents paid a fee to the teacher for the education of their children, and the licensing of teachers was left to the local community. Quite often a minister of a local church examined candidates and issued local certificates, valid only in that community. The chief qualifications were not educational but religious; there were no professional schools, as such, for preparing teachers. Standards for licensing in those days were low or nonexistent and the examining or approving authority varied from community to community. Sometimes local school boards issued the license. An examination of some sort was usually the only requirement for a license, and the questions asked were very elementary. You may be interested in knowing that the local examination (usually given by a county superintendent) continued on the American scene for a long time—actually well into the 20th Century in many states.

During the colonial period there were, of course, no state school systems; the first state school systems came into being about 1820. Only seven of the 16 states which made up the Union in 1800 had constitutions which even mentioned education. The federal constitution made no mention of education, thus leaving the matter to the states under the language of the 10th Amendment. After 1820, constitutions of the various states began referring to the need for education; later all states ruled that state systems should be established.

The date 1825 is important in teacher education as it marked the beginning of the evolution of state certification procedures. In that year the Ohio legislature provided that county examining officers would examine candidates for teaching and issue certificates. New York in 1841 and Vermont in 1845 required county superintendents of schools to perform these duties, among others. Between 1845 and 1900, teacher certification authority was shared by state and county authorities, being almost completely based on the examination system. New York was the first state (1849) to accept evidence of credit from its normal school (the institution that prepared teachers) as a basis of certification instead of the examination. Even as late as 1900 there were about 3,000 teacher licensing agencies in the United States. Some states still certified local teachers on the basis of examination in 1950.

Currently, all states have centralized teacher certification agencies, usually located in their departments of education; the basis for certification is the successful completion of prescribed and approved college and university programs.

Who Must Have a Certificate?

All professional personnel, in all states, who work in public elementary and secondary schools are required by law or regulation to hold certificates issued by the proper authority, usually the state board of education or the state department of education. Such personnel include teachers, administrators, supervisors, and professional nonteaching personnel such as counselors. Also, in almost all states, kindergarten teachers are required to secure certificates if the kindergarten is supported by public funds. A total of 17 states require nursery school teachers to have state certificates if the schools in which they work are publicly supported. Seven states (Arizona, California, Florida, Iowa, Kansas, Massachusetts, and Missouri) require teachers and administrators in publicly-supported junior colleges to hold certificates.

If you wish to teach in a nonpublic school you should know that approximately half of the states require that teachers at some levels or in some subjects hold state certificates. Nine states require certification of teachers in nonpublic schools only if the schools in which they teach meet all the official requirements of the state department of education. About half of the states have no provision for certifying teachers in nonpublic schools.

The question of licensing for paraprofessionals and teacher aides is being debated. At the moment, only eight states have made provisions for licensing or certifying these people. The probable increase in the number of these types of school personnel doubtlessly will lead to some kind of state control or regulations in the future.

Requirements for Certification

State requirements for the certification of teachers can be summarized under the following categories: (1) general requirements; (2) preparation requirements; and (3) special courses.

General Requirements.   General requirements are those that every person applying for a teaching certificate, regardless of field of specialization, must meet. Common examples of requirements are these: United States citizenship (or oath of intent to become a citizen), license fee, good health, oath of allegiance to the U. S. Constitution, minimum age, recommendation of the college where the person received his teacher preparation, or recommendation of the last employer. Many of the general requirements have been dropped in recent years; the minimum age requirement is one example. Present college preparation requirements have made the listing of this requirement for certification unnecessary. Also, the number of states requiring loyalty oaths has been reduced in recent years. Approximately half of the states now do not require a certification fee.

Preparation Requirements.   Almost all of the states and territories now require persons who apply for a regular elementary or secondary teaching certificate to hold at least a bachelor's degree from a college or university offering an approved teacher education program. All state governments provide guidelines to their colleges and universities regarding the kinds of programs and the nature of programs they may offer. Most bachelor's degree programs for teachers include the following: 35 percent general education—these are courses required of all students regardless of the profession or occupation they choose, courses such as English composition, world literature, science; 35 percent subject specialization—these are courses which provide background knowledge in the subject field in which the person plans to teach, for example, further courses in English and literature for those who hope to be English teachers; 20 percent professional education—these are courses in education, such as child growth and development, techniques of teaching, student teaching; and 10 percent electives—courses the student may choose to take to satisfy his own interests or to further his own talents.

Some states are now requiring a fifth year of college training or a master's degree for teachers who continue to teach. Arizona and California now require the master's degree for all secondary teachers but they are still issuing temporary certificates (valid for one year at a time) for teachers with bachelor's degrees if recommended by a district superintendent of schools. The District of Columbia requires the master's degree for senior high and vocational certification.

For school administrators, the basic requirement is five years of preparation, and 24 states require six years of preparation for school superintendents.

Special Courses. Because teacher certification is a state function, some states add requirements for teachers which are unique or special to that state. Before applying for a certificate in another state, the teacher education graduate should review the course requirements of that state.[1] The states and their required special courses at the time of this writing are: Arizona—state constitution; Louisiana—state history (for elementary teachers only); Nevada—state school law and constitution; Oklahoma—state history; Texas—state and federal governments; Washington—state or Northwest history and government; Wisconsin—cooperatives, that is, groups who band together to increase their purchasing power (for teachers of economics and social studies), and agriculture and conservation (for teachers of science and social studies); Wyoming—state constitution. About half of these eight states will accept certain scores on examinations to test knowledge of these areas, rather than course credit, in meeting these special course requirements.

Types of Certificates Issued

The typical practice used by the 50 state authorities is to issue separate elementary school and high school certificates. Most states, in licensing persons who wish to teach in high schools, issue certificates showing the subjects or fields the person is qualified to teach. For elementary school teachers the usual practice is to issue a certificate valid for grades 1-6 or 1-8. Most teaching certificates are valid for a term of five to ten years, five years being the most usual. Approximately half of the states issue life or permanent certificates.

Certification and the Control of Placement. People in and out of the education profession often want certificates to control placement: they want to be sure that the person who teaches French is prepared to teach French, or the person who

teaches first grade is prepared to teach first grade. But certification is not a good way to overcome the misplacement of a teacher in the long run. For initial placement of the recent college graduate, the recommended job assignment listed on the certificate should be insisted upon. But after a few years, the teacher's interests and education may cause him to be effective in other areas also. As a consequence, narrow certification, for example, to teach only oboe or the flute, confuses the meaning of certification and takes attention away from the true purpose—to assure the public that the person certified is competent and qualified. Appropriate placement—being sure that the person has an appropriate preparation for or the demonstrated abilities to teach a particular subject or grade—is the joint responsibility of the professional, the professional organization, and the school district personnel officer.
officer.

The Number of Different Certificates Issued. A recent study indicated that the various states issued a total of 539 separate certificates, averaging about 11 separate certificates per state. This number of certificates tends to be confusing both to the profession and to the public. Most other professions issue only one legal certificate—a license to practice the profession in the state. This tendency toward multiple certificates in teaching is due in part to the constant development of new specialties or subjects; it is due also in part to the pressure placed by members of an emerging specialty who hold in high regard the status of a special certificate which sets them apart from other teachers.

Withdrawing Certificates. The laws of each of the states spell out the conditions under which a teacher's certificate can be withdrawn. The most common reasons are: extreme, unacceptable personal conduct (gross immorality), lack of ability (incompetence), refusal to submit to authority (insubordination which has been used less and less in recent years), and violation of the law (felony). Other causes mentioned in the laws of some states are abandonment of contract, unprofessional conduct, and negligence. A few state laws specify alcoholism, drug abuse, willful neglect of duty, falsification of credentials, and violation of rules of the board as grounds for withdrawing certificates. Recent court cases have tended to cluster the chief causes around the first two mentioned—immorality and incompetence.

The authority to take away teacher certificates is in the hands of state boards of education, but these boards are required to hold hearings so that evidence relative to a case may be reviewed. The teacher may be represented by a lawyer and can present further evidence in his own behalf. Decisions by state boards of education are subject to the review of superior courts and these courts can reverse the decisions of state boards. Historically, many decisions by boards to take away licenses have been reversed by the courts. Withdrawal of a certificate by a state board is a serious event; usually it results in the person not being able to get another teaching job anywhere.

Reciprocity in Certification

As the American population has become more mobile, one of the most continuing and troubling teacher certification problems has been a lack of reciprocity among the states in issuing certificates to persons prepared in other states. A number of methods have been employed to overcome this problem. One has been the establishment of agreements within a given geographical area (regional reciprocity compacts) wherein a person prepared in one state could teach in a neighboring state having similar standards.

Another method which has been tried is a system of national accreditation, that is, of examining all colleges and universities which prepare teachers using the same standards. The National Council for the Accreditation of Teacher Education (NCATE) was established so that states could have confidence in accepting all credentials from any institution accredited by that agency. However, only about 525 of the 1,200 institutions preparing teachers have become accredited by NCATE. It should be pointed out that those institutions prepare about 80 percent of the new teachers each year. Currently, more than 30 states give considerable weight to credentials from NCATE-accredited institutions; this number will probably grow.

A new mechanism for certification across state lines has been developing since 1969. It is called the Interstate Reciprocity Compact, sponsored by the New York State Education Department. For a state to join the compact, its legislature must pass a carefully worded bill (the same bill in each state) which permits the state board or department of education to enter into formal and legal agreements with other compact states regarding certification. The compact allows the student graduating from an approved program in one member state to receive automatic certification in other member states, if those states have signed mutual agreements regarding the nature of preparation programs.

More than 35 states have now passed this law; as a result reciprocity between and among these states is becoming a reality. Although reciprocity has not been fully realized, at least a teacher transferring from the state where he was prepared to another state now has a good chance that his credentials will be accepted. If the teacher is a graduate of a college approved for teacher education and the college is accredited by NCATE or the appropriate regional accrediting association, that person should have little or no difficulty obtaining state certification in a different state.

Use of Examinations in Certification

There has been a steadily increasing trend in recent years for states to make greater use of examinations in the certification process. This is not the kind of basic examination which was used in the early years of our country for issuing local certificates. In the present case extensive examinations are being used to allow a student the opportunity to show mastery of a given subject without having to take a course for credit. An increasing number of colleges are considering the use of these performance tests if and when reliable tests can be established.

Several states have reported that they use examinations in different ways. California uses the Modern Language Association (MLA) Examination to show skills in a foreign language; it also uses trade and skill examinations for advanced or higher level vocational credentials, and the reading specialist part of the National Teachers' Examination (NTE).[1] Colorado uses proficiency examinations in typewriting and shorthand to qualify for teaching these subjects in high school; it also uses the MLA examinations for persons preparing to teach modern languages. Connecticut also uses the MLA examination. Delaware uses exams to confirm work completed in unaccredited colleges or to make up a lack of not more than six semester hours to qualify for a major teaching field if the applicant has had three years teaching experience in the field; it also uses the MLA examination. Hawaii uses the Miller Analogy Test (MAT) and the National Teachers' Examination (NTE) to assure the quality of preparation in unaccredited colleges. Maine allows up to six semester hours in education on the basis of the NTE for the renewal of certificates instead of course credit. New Hampshire uses the MLA examination. New Jersey allows students prepared in other countries to validate work in institutions in their own countries through examinations. The New York State Education Department probably makes the most extensive use of examinations in connection with certification: in cooperation with colleges and universities of the state, college graduates who lack certain courses required for certification may show proficiency in these courses by means of an examination.[2]

All states now have established at the state level advisory councils or commissions on teacher education and certification. These councils are made up of members of the teaching profession and have been established to help state departments of education in developing sound certification policies in keeping with the needs of the schools. Many have established certification review committees to review decisions made by the legal authorities on whether credentials in given cases meet state laws and regulations. Both of these processes tend to offset unreasonable, one-sided decision-making, to give the profession more authority in decision-making, and to further democratize the administration of teacher education and certification.

Possible Future Requirements for Teachers

One can guess that because the teacher shortage is said to be over and a surplus of teachers is available in the manpower pool, either minimum requirements for certification will be raised or admission requirements into teacher preparation programs will be increased—or both. Some states already require a fifth year of college preparation for regular certification; this practice may become more widespread and be adopted by many more states.

It would appear, however, that admission to teacher preparation programs will be more difficult. Already some state legislatures are calling for quotas, that is, the establishment of a maximum number of persons to be prepared at state expense. Some colleges, working cooperatively with professional organization and school district representatives, are establishing stiffer admission procedures: raising academic grade point averages, developing more strict interview procedures, requiring the student to take a battery of tests which are supposed to give evidence of proficiency in academic skills and knowledge, and requiring some type of field-based experience in which a student gains a better understanding of the theory and practice aspects of education. Most colleges are providing students with the facts about supply and demand (as we are providing in this book), not to discourage a person who wants to be a teacher from being one but rather to help the student be aware of what he will be facing after graduation.

Many colleges and universities are developing competency-based or performance-based teacher education programs. These types of programs characteristically include a definition of the specific behaviors (performances) the person in training will be required to demonstrate before he can successfully complete the program. Because the required performances are clearly defined, the materials and circumstances which help the student learn how to perform are also clearly defined. The materials usually are arranged so that the student who uses them will have to display his talents and produce some visible evidence of accomplishment. In learning to teach by doing the work of the teacher "out in the open," where other students in training and the training faculty can both view and help, the student soon learns to give and take constructive suggestions about his work. You should not be surprised if, after you enter a teacher education program, you are faced with competency-based materials and experiences.

Students already in college probably don't need to worry about changes in requirements. Changes in college or certificate requirements never go back to a past date; the college catalog or bulletin which outlined the available courses and programs when you entered serves as an informal contract between you and your college. In effect, it means that if you wish to go ahead with a program outlined therein, the college must honor your intention.

In a similar vein, many people who are actively in the field of education worry about changes in certificate requirements. State authorities can place higher standards for preparation and certification but, again, not going back to a past date. These changes apply only to new people entering teaching.

New Views in Certification

As education has become a major expense of state government more and more legislators have become interested in teacher certification. A few states have established new teacher education and certification commissions, some independent of the state board or state department of education, some directly under the state board. In almost all cases a larger percentage of members of these commissions are practicing classroom teachers.

Practicing classroom teachers and the organizations representing them, such as the National Education Association and the American Federation of Teachers, are seeking more control of certification. This is because certification decisions control entrance into teaching and teachers feel they have as much right to control the number and the competence of those entering teaching as do physicians, lawyers, architects, and other professional groups. In adopting a "Bill of Teacher Rights," the NEA indicated under Article I, Rights as a Professional, "As a member of the teaching profession the individual teacher has the right: (Section 1) To be licensed under professional and ethical standards established, maintained, and enforced by the profession."[3]

You may be interested in knowing that the processes used in issuing teaching certificates have changed only recently. Just a few years ago, applicants had to give transcripts of their college work to the state education agency. There a clerk would check course titles and credits against a master list of courses required for certification. If a person's record included all the required credits in the re-quired courses, the certificate would be issued. Now almost all states are on the "Approved Programs Ap-proach" to certification; that is, if a college's program is approved by the state authority, the person who graduates and is recommended for certification by the college is issued a certificate automatically. As suggested earlier, some states are urging colleges and public schools to work together to provide teacher preparation which is based on demonstrated competence with students in real schools. In these situations persons preparing to teach would have to perform or accomplish tasks according to goals which were stated and agreed to beforehand. Instead of being issued a certificate based on a combination of courses, the person seeking certification would have to provide evidence of excellence of teaching performance in some form, for example, video-tapes or observational records. Effective performance-based or competency-based teacher education is dependent on the availability of reliable means to measure skills, which have not yet been created. Since the development of such instruments through research and experimentation takes so long, we would predict that it will be a long time before complete competency- or performance-based programs are widespread.

Notes

1. See Research Division, National Education Association, *Status of the American Public-School Teacher, 1970-71*, Research Report 1972-R3 (Washington, D.C.: The Association, 1972). See also T. M. Stinnett, *A Manual on Standards Affecting School Personnel in the United States.* Washington, D.C.: National Education Association, 1974.

2. See *College Proficiency Examinations* (Albany, N.Y.: New York State Education Department, n.d.).

3. *NEA Reporter*, "NEA Bill of Teacher Rights," October 1973, XII, No. 5; 8.

The Personal Qualities
of the Teacher

9

"No matter what the subject matter, what the teacher ultimately teaches is himself." What do these words mean to you? As you think about a teacher you've had at any time in the past, what do you recall that he taught you? Do you remember most the subject matter, his personality, or perhaps a combination of both?

What Is an Effective Teacher?

For probably as long as teachers have been in existence there has been the attempt to describe or define "the effective teacher" or "the good teacher." The hope has been that, if such a definition could be developed, selection into teacher education programs and hiring in school systems could be simplified, improved, and, perhaps, even perfected. So far such a definition has not been developed; characteristics have been identified and listed, but the secret of an effective teacher seems to lie in the unique way(s) in which that man or woman combines those characteristics within himself and uses them outwardly in communication and interaction with students. It is understandable that, since learning is a highly individual and personal experience, aiding others to learn must be individual and personal in order to be effective. A good teacher needs not only to understand people in general and individuals in particular but also needs to be creative enough to develop ways and means to help them learn.

Can you list three or four qualities which you feel are essential in a good teacher? As we indicated earlier, in a study based on the opinions of nearly 4,000 high school seniors, the most frequently mentioned reasons for liking a teacher best were (1) helpful in schoolwork, explains lessons and assignments clearly and thoroughly and uses examples in teaching, (2) cheerful, happy, good-natured, jolly, has sense of humor, and can take a joke, (3) human, friendly, companionable, "one of us," (4) interested in and understands pupils.[1] It is immediately apparent that these four most important chacteristics are all closely related to *the person of the teacher* and the way(s) he communicates and interacts with students.

There is no question that teaching, as one of the helping professions, is highly related to people. Therefore, students who enter teaching hoping to be happy and successful in the work of teaching need to be able to relate to people. They need to be the kinds of students who view themselves and others confidently and favorably—who have a positive attitude toward life.

Arthur Combs, in a research study of effective helpers, found that such people viewed others as able, friendly, worthy, dependable, trustworthy, helpful, and important. They saw *themselves* as adequate, trustworthy, wanted by others, worthy, and identified with rather than set apart from others.[2] To state it simply, Combs' effective helpers viewed themselves and others positively and managed to convey this positive feeling to those with whom they worked.

In Chapter 4, the necessity for initiative, creativity, and openness on the part of the teacher was discussed. This "openness" is both an inner dimension and an outer dimension; that is, the *person* (inner part) of the teacher cannot be separated from the *profession* (outer part) of the teacher. The teacher who is open realizes that the true teaching-learning process is a reciprocal process at all times. Ross Mooney illustrates this idea of openness: in order for a person to continue to grow, he must continually interact with the environment; that is, take advantage of every teaching/learning opportunity provided by the persons, places, and things around him, bringing back to his person all that happens in the way of awarenesses and experiences.[3] Such openness allows for, in fact requires, constant growth. Can you identify people in whom this kind of openness, growth, and aliveness exists? Have some of them been your teachers, and have they stimulated you as a student? How do they compare to others whom you may view as having "settled in"? Can you capture the process of openness? Could you help your students to capture it, if you were to become a teacher? How might you go about it?

Being an Effective Person

If you agree with the quote which opened this chapter, ". . . what the teacher ultimately teaches is himself," you may realize that your development as an effective teacher depends on your development as an effective person. Understanding yourself as thoroughly as possible is a beginning—understanding who you are, what you value in life, where you are now, where you want to go, and exploring possible means for getting there. Different people discover answers to these questions in different ways—your way of discovery, your process, may be as important or more important than the end result, the product, because the process tells you something more about yourself.

For instance, you may choose to use the process of counseling for self-understanding. You may contact someone whom you respect, and indicate that you're interested in being a counselee or client. Working together with that person for a period of time would help you discover or rediscover something for yourself which would be helpful to you personally and professionally.

You may choose to read books such as Notes to Myself by Hugh Prather[4] or works of Teilhard de Chardin, such as The Future of Man,[5] and spend hours mulling these over in your mind to decide what applications and implications they have for you. In other words, the process you use may be an individual and private one, rather than the previously mentioned one in which you ask for another person's direct information or experience.

A third option would be taking a battery of personality inventories to develop further insight regarding the type of person you are, compared with some average group. In order for this to be helpful to you, the tests would need to be interpreted by someone who knows you and knows the tests.

Still another option would be participation in some type of group work or group experience. Through group experience, you may give and receive feedback or reactions regarding ways in which you and other members see one another as individuals and group members.

These are only a few possible ways for finding out more about yourself; you may utilize one, several, or a combination. You may be able to think of several more. The important thing is that you use *some* means and be aware of why you choose the process you do because that will give you more useful information about yourself. After you have selected one or more processes for developing self-understanding, ask yourself: Did I choose a method which requires contact with a professional, perhaps, because I value or feel I need or want help from someone who I think knows more than I do about people? Did I choose a method which relies only on my own personal evaluation, perhaps, because I trust my own judgment more than others? Did I choose a method which involves feedback from several people because I want variety, or perhaps because I like more public interaction? The process or processes you choose can tell you as much about yourself as the information you get from others, if you remain open to what you learn.

Developing a fuller understanding of yourself and your own motives is an essential step toward becoming an effective helper for others, as being an effective helper means separating yourself and your own needs and wants, at least temporarily, from the needs and wants of others. To be helpful a person should know himself and be ready to give of his unique talents. This brings us to the next step—what you do with what you have learned about yourself. What decisions does this bring about? What action will you take as a result of what you've learned? Where do you go from here?

Where Do I Go From Here?

This is the stage at which some people stop, because the process may make them uneasy about what they've learned.

Once a person finds out or rediscovers something about himself it may mean that he will need to make some changes in order to be effective in work or in life. And, strangely enough, it may be just as threatening to discover positive things about yourself as it is to discover negative things. For with the acceptance of positive qualities may come higher expectations of yourself that you may or may not wish to accept. Abraham Maslow discusses this in *The Farther Reaches of Human Nature* in a section entitled "The Jonah Complex."[6] With the acceptance of negative qualities may come disappointment or frustration with yourself or with others who give you negative reactions. The truth is that there is some of both elements in all people—increased self-understanding will bring about awareness of some strengths and also some weaknesses.

Here is where the person of the effective helper enters in. As indicated earlier, effective helpers see themselves as adequate and worthy, rather than inadequate and unworthy. Such people, then, will be apt to respond to both positive and negative information about themselves with feelings such as, "I've accomplished some things, I'll keep trying to do the best I can, and I'll find ways to improve the things I need to improve," rather than, for example, "I've really never accomplished much, anyhow; I'll never be good enough. I might as well give up."

The things people say to themselves or the feelings they have about themselves and others are very important, for they form the basis for the ways in which they view themselves and others. And these perceptions form the basis for behavior—people tend to behave in certain ways, based on what they believe to be true. If they believe that they are adequate and worthy, and see others as adequate and worthy, they will tend to behave in ways which indicate these feelings. They will treat others as adequate and worthy.

Do you see the chain of events which this type of understanding, these perceptions, and behaviors can produce in teachers and in the students with whom they work? Can you see the relationship between a teacher's feelings about himself and the rapport a teacher may develop or fail to develop with students? Do you see the importance of *the person of the teacher?*

Teachers can be and often are extremely important people in students' lives. They are in close contact with young people during the growing, years. It is essential that people who enter teaching understand and like themselves, understand and like students, those with whom they work, and their jobs, and have positive outlooks on life. It is important that you give some time and attention to the study of these dimensions in yourself, if you are considering the prospect of becoming a teacher.

Notes

1. Don E. Hamachek, *Encounters with the Self.* (New York: Holt, Rinehart and Winston, Inc., 1971) p. 195.

2. Arthur Combs, Donald L. Avila, William W. Purkey, *Helping Relationships—Basic Concepts for the Helping Professions.* (Boston: Allyn and Bacon, Inc., 1971) pp. 11-16.

3. Ross Mooney, "Cultural and Emotional Blocks to Creative Activity." Paper presented for Engineer Research and Development Laboratories, Fort Belvoir, Virginia, 1955.

4. Hugh Prather, *Notes to Myself.* (Lafayette, Calif.: Real People Press, 1970).

5. Teilhard de Chardin, *The Future of Man.* (New York: Harper and Row, 1969).

6. Abraham Maslow, *The Farther Reaches of Human Nature.* (New York: Viking Press, 1971).

Glossary

Accreditation—a process in which faculty members of other institutions evaluate the program of a school. Accreditation is conducted by associations of institutions and is their way of being sure that a member school is offering quality programs to students.

Affective Learning—the learning of feelings, attitudes and appreciations through experience.

Alternative Schools—schools designed to provide an option to traditional schools. They are often founded by a group of parents or teachers who are interested in emphasizing greater creativity and social sensitivity, nature study, arts and crafts in a school setting.

Cognitive Learning—the learning of knowledge, facts, information, concepts and understandings through experience.

Community—a group of people with a common interest or a common purpose (usually living near one another); people who share their interests and problems with others in the same group. Communities may become formally organized to achieve a goal considered important to the group. Usually, however, communities continue in time and are held together through informal communication networks, networks composed of friends, neighbors, fellow club members, church members, or professional and occupational associates.

Community College—a college serving the educational needs of high school graduates and adults in a region. Community colleges usually offer the first two years of college, plus those vocational, technical and adult education classes which are desired by adults in a service area.

Differentiated Staff—a way of organizing a teaching team so that there are different roles and responsibilities for different members. For example, instead of having a team composed of teachers with equal or parallel roles, a team may have a lead teacher, teacher members, and paraprofessional members; each role will require different responsibilities. In most differentiated staffs, the lead teacher receives a higher salary than the teacher members.

Early Experiencing—activities which call for the college student to work in the elementary or secondary schools or social agencies prior teaching.

Free Schools—places where instruction is provided free or inexpensively outside a regular public or private school. Free school teachers are usually volunteers who teach subjects not included in the regular school curriculum.

Individualized Instruction—a procedure aimed at providing a unique program for every child, with emphasis on differences and diversity. It attempts to more adequately attend to the many differences in students' physical, social, emotional, and psychomotor development.

Inservice Education—teacher training which occurs after the teacher is employed and on the job; may be provided by the employing school system primarily to keep them abrest of changes.

Microteaching—a technique which usually involves videotaping a short lesson (5-10 minutes), playing it back, critiquing it and repeating the operation to improve the instruction. Its primary use is in the preservice education of teachers and the improvement of teachers' skills.

Middle School—a school containing the middle grades, often 5 through 8, and organized to help intermediate age children to explore a wide range of academic and vocational interests.

Montessori Schools—pre- or elementary schools organized to teach basic learning skills (reading, writing, organizing) to young children using carefully structured methods; based on the work of Dr. Maria Montessori during the early years of this century in Italy.

Nongraded Schools—a method of grouping students according to their needs or interests rather than by age or grade. In nongraded schools students can progress at their own rate, moving to more advanced material when they are ready.

Open School—a type of school which provides opportunities for children to pursue their own individual interests at their own rates. In open schools teachers must be able to find materials and design activities which encourage children to use their personal interests and talents constructively.

Paraprofessional—a person trained to serve as a teacher aide or teacher assistant. Normally paraprofessionals carry out specific duties under the direct supervision of the classroom teacher. A paraprofessional may take attendance, collect lunch money, mark papers, type and duplicate materials, listen to children recite, or do any of a number of specific duties that teachers do. A paraprofessional, however, is not responsible for the overall program of instruction provided in the classroom.

Performance Contracting—a procedure by which a school system may contract with a business to perform a specific instructional task such as improving the teaching of spelling. The company or business guarantees to produce specific results in a specific period of time. The term may also be applied to a written agreement between a student and a teacher, in which a student and teacher agree upon a certain amount of work as acceptable for a particular grade.

Positive Reinforcement—a strategy used by teachers to encourage students to learn. When a student does something in a way considered appropriate by the teacher, the teacher praises or rewards the student. Such actions (responses) by a teacher in effect tell a student what he should do. The teacher's actions, therefore, reinforce or support the actions of the student positively, thus the term positive reinforcement.

Preservice Education—the education of the teacher (teacher training) which occurs before his first regular teaching job.

Programed Learning—the use of materials and experiences in a carefully organized sequence in order to produce a change in response or behavior. It usually involves the use of teaching machines, programed texts, and computers.

Psychomotor Learning—through experience the learning of skills, movement and coordinated muscle activity.

Roleplaying—a way of simulating reality in which participants can act out situations for the purpose of discovering alternative solutions to real-life problems.

Shadowing—following a person throughout the day to see what he does, whom he talks to, and what activities he engages in. Shadowing is a good way to learn how another person sees the world.

Simulation—a teaching technique using a model of a real system to provide a realistic representation to stimulate and aid learning. Games, roleplaying, films, and filmstrips are examples of media which may be used in simulation.

Staff Development—a term used to include all of teacher education, preservice and inservice, as well as the training of principals, superintendents, custodians, bus drivers and other school employees. Staff development is the education and training undertaken by a school staff to improve its ability to perform.

Student Teaching—part of a teacher education program which requires the college student to work in the schools full time and to assume, under the supervision of the regular classroom teacher, the duties and responsibilities of the teacher.

Teacher Aides (See *Paraprofessionals*)

Team Teaching—a way of organizing faculty so that a group of students is taught by a team of two or more teachers. The teachers on a team must work very closely together so that their instruction is coordinated. The main advantage of team teaching is that teachers can use their individual talents better. If a member of a teaching team is particularly good in science, whenever a science lesson is planned that member can conduct the lesson while the other team members help.

Suggested Readings

Adams, Sam and J. L. Garrett, *To Be A Teacher: An Introduction to Education.* Englewood Cliffs, N.J.: Prentice-Hall, Inc., 1969.

Anderson, Margaret, *Children of the South.* New York: Dell Publishing Co., 1966.

Anderson, Robert H., *Teaching in a World of Change.* New York: Harcourt, Brace & World, 1966.

Ashton-Warner, Sylvia, *Teacher.* New York: Simon & Schuster, 1963.

Association for Supervision and Curriculum Development. *Evaluation and Feedback As A Guide.* 1967 Yearbook. Washington, D. C.: The Association, 1967.

———, *Perceiving, Behaving, Becoming.* 1962 Yearbook. Washington, D. C.: The Association, 1962.

Axline, Virginia M., *Dibs in Search of Self.* New York: Ballantine Books, Inc., 1969.

Barth, Roland S., *Open Education and the American School.* New York: Schocken Books, 1974.

Baruch, Dorothy, *One Little Boy.* New York: Dell Publishing Co., n.d.

Bennis, Warren G. et al., eds. *The Planning of Change.* (2nd ed.) New York: Holt, Rinehart, & Winston, 1969.

Bettelheim, Bruno. *Love Is Not Enough.* New York: Avon Books, 1971.

Biegeleisen, Jacob I. *Careers and Opportunities in Teaching.* New York: E. P. Dutton, 1969.

Blount, Nathan S. and Herbert J. Klausmeier, *Teaching in the Secondary School.* (3rd ed.) New York: Harper & Row, 1968.

Borton, Terry, *Reach, Touch and Teach.* New York: McGraw-Hill Book Co., Inc., 1970.

Boy, Angelo, *Expanding the Self: Personal Growth for Teachers.* Issues and Innovations in Education Series. Dubuque, Ia.: William C. Brown Co., 1971.

Brenton, Myron, *What's Happened to Teacher?* New York: Avon Books, 1971.

Brown, Claude, *Manchild in the Promised Land.* New York: New American Library, 1971.

Brown, Duane, *Changing Student Behavior: A New Approach to Discipline.* Issues and Innovations in Education Series. Dubuque, Ia.: William C. Brown Co., 1971.

Brubaker, Dale L., *The Teacher as a Decision-Maker.* Dubuque, Ia.: William C. Brown Co., 1970.

Castillo, Gloria, *Left-Handed Teaching: Lessons in Affective Education,* New York: Praeger Publishers, 1974.

Chandler, B. J. et al., *Education and the New Teacher.* New York: Dodd, Mead & Co., 1971.

Clayton, Thomas E., *Teaching and Learning: A Psychological Perspective.* Englewood Cliffs, N. J.: Prentice-Hall, Inc., 1965.

Collier, Calhoun C. et al., *Teaching in the Modern Elementary School.* New York: The Macmillan Co., 1967.

Conant, James B., *The Education of American Teachers.* New York: McGraw-Hill Book Co., 1963.

Corwin, Ronald G., *Militant Professionalism: A Study of Organizational Conflict in High Schools.* New York: Appleton-Century-Crofts, 1970.

Cuban, Larry, *To Make a Difference: Teaching in the Inner City.* New York: Free Press, 1970.

Decker, Sunny, *An Empty Spoon.* New York: Harper & Row, 1969.

Denues, Celia, *Career Perspective: Your Choice of Work.* Worthington, O.: Charles A. Jones Publishing Co., 1972.

De Young, Chris A. and Richard Wynn, *American Education: Foundations in Education.* (7th ed.) New York: McGraw-Hill Book Co., 1972.

Dinkmeyer, Don and Rudolph Dreikurs, *Encouraging Children to Learn: The Encouragement Process.* Englewood Cliffs, N. J.: Prentice-Hall, Inc., 1963.

Dizney, Henry F., *Classroom Evaluation for Teachers.* Issues and Innovations in Education Series. Dubuque, Ia.: William C. Brown Co., 1971.

Dreeben, Robert, *The Nature of Teaching: Schools and the Work of Teachers.* Glenview, Ill.: Scott, Foresman and Co., 1970.

Dropkin, Stan et al., *Contemporary American Education: An Anthology of Issues, Problems, Challenges.* (2nd ed.) New York: The Macmillan Co., 1970.

Encyclopedia of Educational Research. (4th ed.) "Economic Status," pp. 334-35; "Teacher Effectiveness," pp. 1429-34; "Teacher Certification," pp. 1410-13; "Student Teaching," pp. 1379-80; "Team Teaching," pp. 562-63; "Teacher Education Programs," 1415-20; "Collective Action," (organization) pp. 154-60. New York: The Macmillan Co., 1969.

Engelmann, Siegfried and Therese Engelmann, *Preventing Failure in the Primary Grades*. Chicago: Science Research Associates, 1969.

Erickson, Erik H., *Childhood and Society*. (rev. ed.) New York: Norton Co., 1964.

Ernst, Kenneth, *Games Students Play: And What to Do About Them*. Milbrae, Calif.: Celestial Arts Publishing Co., 1972.

Fox, Robert, Margaret Luszki, and Richard Schmuck, *Diagnosing Classroom Learning Environments*. Chicago: Science Research Associates, 1966.

Frankl, Victor E., *Man's Search for Meaning*. New York: Beacon Press, 1963.

Fromm, Erich, *The Art of Loving*. New York: Harper & Row, 1974.

Furth, Hans G., *Piaget for Teachers*. Englewood Cliffs, N.J.: Prentice-Hall, Inc., 1970.

Gattman, Eric and William Henricks, *The Other Teacher: Aides to Learning*. Belmont, Calif.: Wadsworth Publishing Co., 1973.

Ginsberg, Eli et al., *The Middle Class Negro in the White Man's World*. New York: Columbia University Press, 1969.

Goodlad, John I., M. Frances Klein and Associates, *Looking Behind the Classroom Door*. Worthington, O.: Charles A. Jones Publishing Co., 1974.

Goslin, David A., *The School in Contemporary Society*. Chicago: Scott, Foresman and Co., 1965.

Greer, Mary and Bonnie Rubinstein, *Will the Real Teacher Please Stand Up: A Primer in Humanistic Education*. Pacific Palisades, Calif.: Goodyear Publishing Co., 1972.

Gronlund, Norman E., *Constructing Achievement Tests*. Englewood Cliffs, N.J.: Prentice-Hall, Inc., 1968.

Gross, Ronald, ed., *The Teacher and the Taught*. New York: Dell Publishing Co., 1963.

Hamachek, D. E., *Encounters With Self*. New York: Holt, Rinehart & Winston, Inc., 1971.

Haney, John B. and Eldon Ullmer, *Educational Media and the Teacher*. Issues and Innovations in Education Series. Dubuque, Ia.: William C. Brown Co., 1970.

Harmin, Merrill and Thomas B. Gregory, *Teaching Is . . . .* Chicago: Science Research Associates, 1974.

Haskew, Lawrence D. and Jonathon C. McLendon, *This Is Teaching: Foundations of American Education.* Chicago: Scott, Foresman and Co., 1968.

Hentoff, Nat, *Our Children Are Dying.* New York: Viking Press, 1970.

Herr, Selma E., *Learning Activities for Reading.* (2nd ed.) Dubuque, Ia.: William C. Brown Co., 1971.

Hersey, John, *The Child Buyer.* New York: Bantam Books, 1971.

Hertzberg, Alvin and Edward F. Stone, *Schools Are for Children: An American Approach to the Open Classroom.* New York: Schocken Books, 1971.

Hipple, Theodore W., *Crucial Issues in Contemporary Education.* Pacific Palisades, Calif.: Goodyear Publishing Co., 1973.

Humphreys, Alice Lee, *Heaven in My Hand.* Atlanta, Ga.: John Knox Press, 1964.

Hymes, James L., Jr., *Teaching the Child Under Six.* Education-Elementary Series. (2nd ed.) Columbus, O.: Charles E. Merrill, 1974.

Jencks, Christopher, *Inequality: A Reassessment of the Effect of Family and Schooling in America.* New York: Harper & Row, 1973.

Johnson, David W., *Reaching Out: Interpersonal Effectiveness and Self-Actualization.* Englewood Cliffs, N.J.: Prentice-Hall, Inc., 1972.

Kaplan, Sandra N. et al., *Change for Children.* Pacific Palisades, Calif.: Goodyear Publishing Co., 1973.

Kaufman, Bel, *Up the Down Staircase.* Englewood Cliffs, N.J.: Prentice-Hall, Inc., 1964.

Kohl, Herbert, *Thirty-Six Children.* New York: New American Library, 1973.

Konopka, Gisela, *The Adolescent Girl in Conflict.* Englewood Cliffs, N.J.: Prentice-Hall, Inc., 1966.

Kozol, Jonathan, *Death at an Early Age. The Destruction of the Hearts and Minds of Negro Children in the Boston Public Schools.* New York: Bantam Books, 1970.

Kvaraceus, William C., *Dynamics of Delinquency.* Columbus, O.: Charles E. Merrill, 1966.

Leacock, Eleanor B., *Teaching and Learning in City Schools.* New York: Basic Books, Inc., 1969.

Lenski, Gerhard, *Power and Privilege: A Theory of Social Stratification.* New York: McGraw-Hill Book Co., 1966.

Leonard, George B., *Education and Ecstasy.* New York: Dell Publishing Co., 1968.

Maslow, Abraham H., ed., *Motivation and Personality.* (2nd ed.) Harper & Row, 1970.

Michael, Donald N., *The Next Generation: The Prospects Ahead for the Youth of Today and Tomorrow.* New York: Random House, 1965.

Miel, Alice and Edwin Kiester, Jr., *The Shortchanged Children of Suburbia: What Schools Don't Teach About Human Differences and What Can Be Done About It.* Old Bethpage, N.Y.: Institute of Human Relations Press, 1967.

Moustakas, Clark, *Creativity and Conformity.* New York: Van Nostrand Reinhold Co., 1967.

_____, *The Authentic Teacher: Sensitivity and Awareness in the Classroom.* Cambridge, Mass.: Howard A. Doyle Publishing Co., 1969.

National Education Association. *Conditions of Work for Quality Teaching.* Washington, D. C.: The Association of Classroom Teachers, 1959.

Nelson, Lois N., ed., *The Nature of Teaching.* Lexington, Mass.: Xerox College Publishers, 1969.

Noar, Gertrude, *Teacher Aides at Work.* Washington, D. C.: National Education Association, 1967.

Overly, Donald E., Jon Rye Kinghorn and Richard Preston, *The Middle School: Humanizing Education for Youth.* Worthington, O.: Charles A. Jones Publishing Co., 1972.

Perkinson, Henry J., *The Imperfect Panacea: American Faith in Education, 1865-1965.* New York: Random House, 1968.

Perrone, Philip, T. Antoinette Ryan and Franklin R. Zeran, *Guidance and the Emerging Adolescent.* New York: Intext Publishers, 1970.

Prather, Hugh, *Notes to Myself.* Moab, Utah: Real People Press, 1970.

Pullias, Earl V. and James D. Young, *A Teacher Is Many Things.* Bloomington, Ind.: Indiana University Press, 1968.

Raths, James E., John R. Pancella and James S. Van Ness, *Studying Teaching.* (2nd ed.) Englewood Cliffs, N. J.: Prentice-Hall, Inc., 1971.

Read, Katherine H., *The Nursery School: A Human Relationships Laboratory.* (5th ed.) Philadelphia: W. B Saunders Co., 1971.

Richey, Robert W., *Planning for Teaching.* (4th ed.) New York: McGraw-Hill Book Co., 1973.

_____, *Preparing for a Career in Teaching: Challenges, Changes, and Issues.* New York: McGraw-Hill Book Co., 1974.

Russell, Ivan L., *Motivation.* Issues and Innovations in Education Series. Dubuque, Ia.: William C. Brown Co., 1974.

Schmuck, Richard A. and Patricia A. Schmuck, *Group Processes in the Classroom.* Issues and Innovations in Education Series. Dubuque, Ia.: William C. Brown Co., 1970.

Schreiber, Daniel, ed., *Profile of the School Dropout.* New York: Random House, 1968.

Schutz, William C., *Joy: Expanding Human Awareness.* New York: Grove Press, Inc., 1967.

Shostrom, Everett L., *Man, the Manipulator.* New York: Bantam Books, 1968.

Shumsky, Abraham, *In Search of Teaching Style.* Englewood Cliffs, N.J.: Prentice-Hall, Inc., 1968.

Silberman, Charles E., *Crisis in the Classroom.* New York: Random House, 1970.

Simon, Sidney B., Leland W. Howe and Howard Kirschenbaum, *Values Clarification: A Handbook of Practical Strategies for Teachers and Students.* New York: Hart Publishing Co., 1972.

Stinnett, T. M., *Turmoil in Teaching: A History of the Organizational Struggle for American Teachers.* New York: The Macmillan Co., 1968.

Stinnett, T. M., *A Manual on Standards Affecting School Personnel in the United States.* Washington, D.C.: National Education Association, 1974.

_____, *The Profession of Teaching.* New York: Center for Applied Research in Education, Inc., 1962.

_____, *Professional Problems of Teachers.* (3rd ed.) New York: The Macmillan Co., 1968.

_____, ed., *The Teacher Dropout.* Itasca, Ill.: F.E. Peacock Publishers, Inc., 1970.

————, ed., *The Unfinished Business of the Teaching Profession in the 1970's.* Bloomington, Ind.: Phi Delta Kappa, 1970.

Strom, Robert, *The Urban Teacher: Selection, Training and Supervision.* Columbus, Ohio: Charles E. Merrill Publishing Co., 1971.

Torrance, E. Paul, *Encouraging Creativity in the Classroom.* Issues and Innovations in Education Series. Dubuque, Ia.: William C. Brown, 1970.

Van Til, William, *Education: A Beginning.* Boston: Houghton-Mifflin Co., 1971.

Von Haden, Herbert I. and Jean Marie King, *Educational Innovator's Guide.* Worthington, Ohio: Charles A. Jones Publishing Co., 1974.

Von Haden, Herbert I. and Jean Marie King, *Innovations in Education: Their Pros and Cons.* (4th ed.) Worthington, Ohio: Charles A. Jones Publishing Co., 1971.

Weigand, James E., ed., *Developing Teaching Competencies.* Englewood Cliffs, N.J.: Prentice-Hall, Inc., 1971.

Weinberg, Meyer, *Integrated Education: A Reader.* Beverly Hills, Calif: The Glencoe Press, 1968.

Wittmer, Joe and Robert D. Myrick, *Facilitative Teaching: Theory and Practice.* Pacific Palisades, Calif.: Goodyear Publishing Co., 1973.

Index

The Authors

T. M. Stinnett has long been associated with the preparation of teachers. He was director of the division of teacher education and certification in his native Arkansas and served for 10 years as executive secretary of the National Commission on Teacher Education formed by the National Education Association. Among many other authoritative writings on the teaching profession, Dr. Stinnett has been responsible for compiling and updating the primary source book on legal requirements for educators, first issued in 1951 as *A Manual on Certification Requirements for School Personnel in the United States* and most recently revised and published under the title *A Manual on Standards Affecting School Personnel in the United States*. Dr. Stinnett was assistant executive secretary of the NEA for six years. He is now on the faculty of the College of Education, Texas A&M University.

William H. Drummond is a professor of education in the Division of Curriculum and Instruction, College of Education, University of Florida. A veteran of elementary and secondary teaching in both public and private schools, Dr. Drummond also served as associate for teacher education in the Washington state department of education.

Alice W. Garry is on the staff of the Bernalillo (New Mexico) Mental Health/Mental Retardation Center. Dr. Garry's experience includes 14 years as a classroom teacher; she also served as coordinator of the *Freshman Early Experiencing Program* at The Ohio State University.